Hunger in the Land of Plenty

Hunger in the Land of Plenty

A Critical Look at Food Insecurity

James D. Wright,
Amy Donley, and
Sara Strickhouser Vega

LYNNE
RIENNER
PUBLISHERS

BOULDER
LONDON

Published in the United States of America in 2019 by
Lynne Rienner Publishers, Inc.
1800 30th Street, Boulder, Colorado 80301
www.rienner.com

and in the United Kingdom by
Lynne Rienner Publishers, Inc.
Gray's Inn House, 127 Clerkenwell Road, London EC1 5DB

Library of Congress Cataloging-in-Publication Data
A Cataloging-in-Publication record for this book
is available from the Library of Congress.

ISBN 978-1-62637-765-3

British Cataloguing in Publication Data
A Cataloguing in Publication record for this book
is available from the British Library.

Printed and bound in the United States of America

The paper used in this publication meets the requirements
of the American National Standard for Permanence of
Paper for Printed Library Materials Z39.48-1992.

5 4 3 2 1

*To those who struggle in the face of long odds
to make ends meet, put food on the table, and
keep the wolf away from the door*

Contents

Tables

Acknowledgments

Our first debt of gratitude is to the agencies and organizations that thought well enough of our work to put up the money to support it: the AARP Foundation, the Florida Department of Agriculture and Consumer Services, the Senior Resource Alliance of Central Florida, Seniors First, and the Winter Park Health Foundation. Other agencies that have aided us in this effort by arranging interviews, sharing data, and supporting our work in countless other ways include HOPE Helps of Oviedo, Florida; Second Harvest Food Bank of Central Florida; Women's Residential and Counseling Center; Tuskawilla Presbyterian Church; and Heart of Florida United Way.

Much of the original empirical work that led to this book was done by cohorts of graduate students in the Department of Sociology at the University of Central Florida. It is a pleasure to acknowledge their assistance: Mandi Barringer, J. Dillon Caldwell, Justin Fletcher, Marie C. Gualtieri, Brittany Minnick Hanson, Meghan M. Harte, James McCutcheon, Olivia Metott, Grant Mohi, Rachel E. Morgan, Chelsea Nordham, Brenda Savage, Marc Settembrino, Katelan Smith, and Nate Van Ness.

The book has benefited from countless conversations with colleagues and friends, many of whom also merit mention by name: Harry Barley, Karen Broussard, Bob Brown, Jill Hamilton Buss, Daryl Flynn, Eric Geboff, Elizabeth Grauerholz, Erin Gray, Tom

Horvath, Randy Hunt, Dave Krepcho, Marsha Lorenz, Santos Maldonado, Joan Nelson, Larry Olness, Nicole Owens, Lisa Portelli, Patricia Rice, Diana Silvey, Keith Theriot, Abby Walters, and Walt Willis. Our gratitude to these people is not only for the assistance freely rendered but also for the work they do in our community every day. These are the good people of the earth.

Several anonymous reviewers read previous versions of this book, and the present version owes a great deal to their reactions and suggestions. If any of you are reading the book for a second time, please know how much we benefited from your comments.

We are also grateful for the assistance of Traci Milbuta, Tamara Pullin, and Shannon Cajigas, who manage our office, keep the paperwork flowing, and respond to every crisis with competence and unfailing good cheer. Our deep gratitude also goes to Carrie Broadwell-Tkach, who saw value in the work and shepherded it capably through the Lynne Rienner editorial process.

Finally, we thank our respective families and friends for putting up with us as we fought through the distractions inherent in writing a book.

1

Food Insecurity
in Context

In 1968, during Lyndon Johnson's War on Poverty, CBS Reports aired the documentary "Hunger in America." It was a searing exposé of hunger, malnutrition, and starvation in American society. The documentary reported that there were 10 million hungry people in the United States, about 5 percent of the entire population. With graphic images from Indian reservations, the Mississippi delta, Appalachia, and the black inner city, the documentary revealed to its American television audience malnourished children, sharecroppers sleeping on rat-infested bedding, and migrant workers literally too hungry to move their broken bodies into the field to harvest crops. The report concluded with a plea to "do something" about widespread hunger in the United States.

Half a century has passed since the *CBS Reports* documentary, and hunger in the United States has taken on a new face. The very term "hunger" has receded from the public policy discussion in favor of today's debate about "food insecurity." And instead of 10 million hungry people and a hunger rate of 5 percent, today's food-insecure population is estimated at around 50 million people, or one American in six. This book tells the story of how we managed to get from one in twenty who were hungry to one in six who are food-insecure.

The present chapter situates the problem of hunger or food insecurity in a broader theoretical and global context. We review how the

1

definition of food insecurity has evolved over the past several decades and how the US Department of Agriculture (USDA) came to develop what is now the consensus definition and measurement. We also review survey evidence on the extent of food insecurity in the United States and how that compares to certain other nations. We review both theoretical and empirical evidence that food insecurity is predominantly a problem of how food is accessed and distributed, not a problem of insufficient production. And we also consider how the problem has been framed in the literatures of community organizing, economics, and anthropology.

Subsequent chapters explore the social and demographic correlates of food insecurity (Chapter 2) and the consequences of food insecurity for physical and mental health (Chapter 3). These chapters describe food as a valued commodity that is very unevenly distributed in most contemporary societies; as such, food is the same as money, prestige, influence, well-being, or self-esteem—namely, an important if often overlooked element of inequality, poverty, and social stratification.

Many contemporary discussions of food insecurity and dietary inadequacies point the finger of blame at so-called food deserts, ecological areas that are bereft of healthy food outlets. Chapter 4 reviews the arguments and explains why the focus on food deserts has been somewhat misplaced. In the same vein, Chapter 5 explains why people cannot realistically be expected to solve their own food insecurities. Backyard and community gardens, farmers' markets, food pantries, guerrilla gardens, and many of the other elements of the so-called alternative food movement have a lot to contribute, but they do not constitute a realistic solution to food insecurity.

A great deal of public policy focuses on food insecurity, so much so that many people just assume that food stamps, Meals on Wheels, and the school breakfast and lunch programs have effectively solved the problem. But all of these programs have problems of access and participation that limit their effectiveness, as concluded in Chapter 6.

Experts and organizations from the United Nations (UN) down fear that the world's production of food will need to double in the next few decades if mass starvation is to be avoided. We conclude the book with an extended argument that the earth produces more than enough food to go around and that scientific advances will ensure this truth well into the next century. The problem, to reiterate, is not that there is not enough food but rather that there are gross inefficiencies and inequalities in how the available food gets distributed to the world's population.

This book is intended as a comprehensive overview of a truly vast literature on food, food insecurities, and hunger in the modern world, and as such we have sacrificed depth of detail in many places in favor of wide-ranging summaries of what is presently known. But we have also tried to provide current references that can be consulted for additional details on almost every point we make.

A decade after CBS brought the problem of hunger into the national spotlight, political scientist Ronald Inglehart (1977) published his very influential book *The Silent Revolution*. The book depicted a profound change of values in the advanced Western societies, from "an overwhelming emphasis on material well-being and physical security" (p. 3) to a new emphasis on quality of life. Tellingly, Inglehart wrote that "a desire for beauty may be more or less universal, but hungry people are more likely to seek food than aesthetic satisfaction. Today, an unprecedentedly large portion of Western populations have been raised under conditions of exceptional economic security" (p. 3). He then described the anticipated changes in social and political values that will result from that security. The very basis of political struggle will change, Inglehart predicted, from a focus on economic well-being to a "higher-order" quest for self-actualization and aesthetic and psychological satisfaction.

In 1977, when those words were being written, the official US poverty rate stood at 11.6 percent and the entire poverty population of the nation was around 25 million people. Today (2016 data), the poverty rate is higher, at 12.7 percent, and the poverty population is up to 41 million people (US Census Bureau 2017). The idea that the populations of the advanced Western societies are, or have been, liberated from economic want no longer resonates with the facts. Some have been liberated from material insecurity, but many have not. This book focuses on the latter.

A famous paper published by psychologist Abraham Maslow in 1943 depicted a "hierarchy of needs." At the bottom of the hierarchy were the most basic human physiological needs: breathing, food, water, sex, sleep, homeostasis, and excretion. Just one step up from the bottom were safety needs, then needs for love, community, and belonging, then the need for esteem (confidence, achievement, respect), and finally the need for self-actualization. The general theory (still prominent in sociology, management training, and education but largely supplanted by other theories in psychology) is that needs at lower levels must be satisfied before consciousness is freed to pursue higher-level goals. Inglehart's theory generalizes the "hierarchy of needs" to entire societies and depicts social development as a progression through the hierarchy. Whether Inglehart's depiction is plausible or not, the important point is that people who face obstacles in satisfying their lower-order needs—that is, the food-insecure—may be prevented from pursuing higher-order needs. And this calls attention not just to the incidence and social location of food insecurity but also to its consequences for physical and psychological well-being.

Despite widespread use, there is no universally agreed-upon definition of what it means to be "food-secure" or, indeed, whether "food security" is a property of individuals, families, communities, whole nation-states, or the entire global food production and distribution system. Two decades ago, developmental economist Simon Maxwell (1996) identified thirty-two distinct definitions of food insecurity in the research and policy literature, a number that has since grown. These definitions run the gamut from the crassly bureaucratic to the ennobling: "a basket of food, nutritionally adequate, culturally acceptable, procured in keeping with human dignity and enduring over time" (p. 169). These definitions show an evolution in thinking about food insecurity from a global level to a national level and finally to the level of persons and households; from an initial focus on food to a larger focus on livelihoods (i.e., from "food first" to poverty and political economy); and on the measurement side, from objective indicators (weight, nutritional intake, hunger) to subjective perceptions, as in the now-universal USDA food-insecurity scale discussed later.

"Food insecurity" is a rather sterile euphemism without the emotional impact of terms such as "hunger," "starvation," or "malnourishment." On the global scene, the term made its first official appearance at the 1974 World Food Conference, where it was defined as enough food to sustain steady population growth and stabilize agricultural production and prices. This, obviously, defined food security as a property of entire nation-states. A second World Food Summit, in 1996, redefined food security and insecurity as properties of people and families: food security exists when and where "all people, at all times, have physical and economic access to sufficient, safe and nutritious food to meet their dietary needs and food preferences for an active and healthy life" (International Food Policy Research Institute 2017:1).

In the United States, the USDA has been taking annual measurements of hunger and food insecurity since the 1990s.[1] Prior to 2006, those at the extreme end of the USDA food-insecurity scale were labeled "food insecure with hunger" to indicate households "in which one or more people were hungry at times during the year because they could not afford enough food" (*hunger* was defined as "the uneasy or painful sensation caused by lack of food"). In 2006, the USDA changed the terminology from "food insecure with hunger" to "very low food security," and "hunger" was thus purged from the national discourse. Researchers stopped asking whether people were literally starving, stunted, or underweight and began asking instead whether people had missed meals, were worried about running out of food, were unable to afford nutritious meals, or had ever sent their children to bed hungry. The conceptual shift was away from the experience of hunger and toward the anxieties that resulted from uncertainties about the household food supply.

Today, the USDA defines food insecurity as "the state of being without reliable access to a sufficient quantity of affordable, nutritious food" (US Department of Agriculture 2016). There are four key terms in this definition: access, sufficient quantity, affordable, and nutritious. Of these, affordability has received the most attention. Indeed, the idea that food insecurity results from inadequate economic resources is built into the very questions used to measure the concept. All of the eighteen survey questions that the USDA uses to determine household food insecurity (presented and discussed later and in the appendix to this book) include economic qualifiers— "because there wasn't enough money for food," "because we were running out of money to buy food," "because we couldn't afford" to buy nutritious food, and so on. The USDA measures assume that food insecurity is an economic issue.

But people can be food-insecure for reasons other than lack of money. An emerging literature on "food deserts" suggests that even relatively well-off people can be food-insecure if there is no supermarket close to where they live.[2] And there can also be transportation, mobility, or disability issues that interfere with access to food. The large majority of the US population shops for groceries by car (Morrison and Mancino 2015), and yet one in ten households does not own or have direct access to a car. In some urban areas, the "car-less" are a fourth of the population. Or there may be cultural issues—that is, culturally based preferences for foodstuffs that nearby grocery stores and food outlets don't carry. If the things people want to eat and know how to prepare are unavailable, food insecurity might be the result. Finally, if we take the point about "nutritious food" in the USDA definition seriously, people may be food-insecure because they are not sufficiently knowledgeable about nutrition to purchase healthy foods. Affordability is only one part of a complicated issue, and yet very little of the existing research on food insecurity has addressed any of these complicating factors of mobility limitations, food deserts, cultural issues, or nutritional knowledge, all issues we address in later pages.

Why has "hunger" fallen out of favor in public policy discussions while "food insecurity" has fallen in? There are several reasons, some more obvious than others. First, hunger is a physiological state that is difficult to measure in surveys. Food insecurity is a social, cultural, or economic status and is easier to conceptualize and measure. People can more easily tell you that they are worried about running out of food than they can describe the sensation of being hungry.

Second, saying that people are "hungry" implies a much greater degree of need than saying they have problems with access to food. Hunger became very politicized subsequent to the aforementioned CBS documentary, especially during the Reagan years. Politicization of the issue stimulated a lot of fairly useless controversy over whether Americans were "really hungry"—whether poor people in the United States were as deprived as, say, people in Haiti or Honduras. "Hunger" seems to generate shrill and often inaccurate reactions from across the political spectrum. "Food insecurity" has been an easier concept to accept.

Third, food insecurity describes a much wider although less serious problem than hunger. Even in the days when "hunger" was part of the USDA lexicon, it was reserved for those at the extreme end of the food-insecurity scale. But a family does not need to be at the extreme end to experience occasional issues with securing food. Food insecurity does not necessarily mean hunger any more than poverty implies homelessness. The food-insecure may well be anxious about being hungry, but it is their anxiety that food-insecurity surveys measure.

Still, we should not let public policy euphemisms blind us to the realities of the conditions we study. When low-income children fall asleep in Monday classes because they haven't eaten all weekend, or adult men stand in line at the local soup kitchen for their one hot meal of the day, or seniors line up at the local grocery store because day-old bread is being given away, it is not because they are food-insecure, it is because they are hungry.

Food insecurity has been recognized as a significant public policy problem for two or three decades now. For the last of those decades, the Institute for Social and Behavioral Sciences at the University of Central Florida[3] has been involved in a great deal of research on various aspects of the problem. This book weaves the materials from our research program into a narrative that relates the lessons we have learned.

There is a line in Aleksandr Solzhenitsyn's *One Day in the Life of Ivan Denisovich* that reads: "The belly is an ungrateful wretch, it never remembers past favors, it always wants more tomorrow."[4] This reminds us that while human needs for, say, companionship or self-actualization or aesthetic fulfillment can be satisfied on an occasional basis, the need for food and water is ever-present. A full belly only lasts until it is time to eat again, a few hours or at most a day. "It always wants more tomorrow." And it is the tomorrow of food availability that has put food insecurity on the political agenda.

On History, Definitions, and Measurement

When the concept of food insecurity first entered the public policy lexicon, it was conceived as a property of entire nations. The setting was Rome, the date was 1974, and the occasion was the first World Food Conference convened by the UN's Food and Agricultural Organization (FAO). The conference was convened as a United Nations response to the devastating Bangladesh famine of the previous two years.

UN world summits, conferences, workshops, and the like are often long on high-minded pronouncements but short on concrete plans of action and implementation. In this case, the high-minded pronouncement at the Rome conference was the Universal Declaration on the Eradication of Hunger and Malnutrition, which obligated all nations to accept the principle that

> every man, woman and child has the inalienable right to be free from hunger and malnutrition in order to develop fully and maintain their physical and mental faculties. Society today already

possesses sufficient resources, organizational ability and technology and hence the competence to achieve this objective. Accordingly, the eradication of hunger is a common objective of all the countries of the international community, especially of the developed countries and others in a position to help.

The declaration passed unanimously, but more than forty years have passed and a large share of the world's population, even in the most advanced industrial societies, have yet to see their hunger and food insecurities erased. An inalienable right, perhaps, but an *enforced* right—not so much.

One famous legacy of the 1974 Rome conference was the declaration by then–US secretary of state Henry Kissinger that within ten years no child anywhere in the world would need to go to bed hungry. But in the 2013 Current Population Survey of the US population, 1.3 percent of respondents with children answered yes to the question, "In the last 12 months, were the children ever hungry but you just couldn't afford more food?" and 0.8 percent said yes when asked, "In the last 12 months, did any of the children ever skip a meal because there wasn't enough money for food?" (Coleman-Jenson, Gregory, and Singh 2014). These are American children who continue to "go to bed hungry," not Haitians or Bangladeshis. Kissinger's 1974 declaration was far off the mark.

Proponents of "American exceptionalism" always expect the United States to be different from the rest of the world—more advanced, more affluent, happier, and more secure than any other nation. But in matters such as inequality and poverty, the United States frequently lags behind other advanced democratic nations. Food insecurity is one such case. Problems of access to sufficient food are visible not just in the less developed or so-called emerging nations but also in the most affluent nation in the history of the world.

Is Food Insecurity a Property of Nations, Communities, or Individuals?

The Universal Declaration on the Eradication of Hunger and Malnutrition recognized the distinction between the developed and undeveloped nations and stated that the former should help resolve the hunger issues of the latter. In the declaration, "food security" is explicitly mentioned on five occasions, and usually, within context, the notion is conceived as a property of entire nations. Thus, at that time, Bangladesh and Honduras (along with many others) were food-insecure, whereas Canada, Italy, and the United States (along with many others) were not. The declaration failed to recognize that there could be highly food-insecure persons and households, or even whole communities, inside developed and generally food-secure nations, and that the problem of food insecurity was not confined to the developing world—a theme we stress throughout this volume.

The following Rome World Food Summit of 1996 abandoned the idea that food insecurity was a problem only in the developing economies, although the recognition remained that the developing world was where the problem was most severe. The 1996 Rome Declaration of Food Security pledged "to achieve food security *for all* and to an ongoing effort to eradicate hunger *in all countries,* with an immediate view to reducing the number of undernourished people to half their present level no later than 2015" (emphasis added). The recognition that food insecurity was a problem in all countries was a major conceptual step forward.

In an important passage, the new declaration (at www.fao.org) asserted:

> Poverty is a major cause of food insecurity and sustainable progress in poverty eradication is critical to improve access to food. Conflict, terrorism, corruption and environmental degradation also contribute significantly to food insecurity. Increased food production, including staple food, must be undertaken. This should happen within the framework of sustainable management of natural resources, elimination of unsustainable patterns of consumption and production, particularly in industrialized countries, and early stabilization of the world population. We acknowledge the fundamental contribution to food security by women, particularly in rural areas of developing countries, and the need to ensure equality between men and women. Revitalization of rural areas must also be a priority to enhance social stability and help redress the excessive rate of rural-urban migration confronting many countries.

This passage introduced several key themes into the discussion of food insecurity that remain with us today. Food insecurity is a problem of poverty and unequal income distribution; it is, in short, an element in the social stratification of societies. Large-scale social forces such as corruption and conflict contribute to the problem. A permanent solution will require environmentally sustainable agricultural practices. Overconsumption in the industrialized world creates food insecurities both there and elsewhere. There are important gender and urban-rural aspects to the issue. And food-insecure people and families can be found in all countries, regardless of their economic development.

Enter the US Department of Agriculture

The USDA first surveyed Americans about food insecurity in 1995, with a "food security" supplemental module implemented in the December wave of the 1995 Current Population Survey. This module, now known as the Current Population Survey Food Security Supplement, has been administered annually ever since and serves as the data resource of record for research on food insecurity in the United States.

The USDA's interest in food security originated in the National Nutrition Monitoring and Related Research Act of 1990. The ten-year comprehensive plan developed under the auspices of the act called on the USDA to develop standardized definitions and survey items that could be used to measure food insecurity or food insufficiency. In 1994, following a detailed review of the literature, the USDA's Food and Nutrition Service cosponsored a National Conference on Food Security Measurement and Research, the outcome of which was the now famous eighteen-item Food Security Supplement to the Current Population Survey. Major modifications to the survey to improve data quality and reduce respondent burden were made in 1998, and the survey has been administered annually ever since.

In their current manifestation, the eighteen survey items are listed in the appendix to this book. The appendix also shows the responses obtained in the 2014 survey. We summarize the survey items under three broad topics: item "difficulty" and response metrics; how the eighteen items are scaled; and prevalence of food insecurity in the United States.

Item "Difficulty" and Response Metrics

The eighteen survey items present respondents with a variety of response metrics. Several of the eighteen questions require simple yes/no responses, others ask "how true" a particular statement is, still others ask how often a particular problem or issue occurs. Moreover, some of the items reflect low levels of food insecurity ("We worried whether our food would run out before we got money to buy more"), whereas others indicate more dire circumstances ("In the last 12 months, did you ever not eat for a whole day because there wasn't enough money for food?").

Inevitably, different items suggest very different conclusions about the degree of food insecurity. In 2014, about 20 percent of the US adult population (19.5 percent) said they had worried sometime in the previous year that their food would run out before they got money to buy more, but fewer than 2 percent said they had skipped meals for an entire day. Ditto on the children's questions: 17 percent of respondents with children said they occasionally relied on a few kinds of low-cost food to feed their children, but only 0.1 percent (one respondent in a thousand) reported at least one occasion when their children did not eat for an entire day.

Researchers are used to answering "How many?" questions with some version of "It depends on what you mean." If food insecurity exists when people are worried about running out of food, then the food-insecure fraction of the US population is 19.5 percent. If food insecurity means people have skipped meals because they couldn't afford food, then the food-insecure fraction is less than 2 percent. If someone is food-insecure when they give an insecure response to *any* of the USDA items, the food-insecure fraction is about one in three. But "somewhere between 2 percent and 30 percent" is not a very compelling answer. Policymakers and the public demand a precision that the empirics of data and surveys can rarely satisfy.

To be useful to policymakers and acceptable to the public, something had to be done to the eighteen items to generate a precise answer to the "How many?" question. The USDA responded to this need with a scaling algorithm that has been used ever since.

How the Eighteen Items Are Scaled

To address the incommensurability of response metrics, all the items with responses other than yes/no were recoded to some sort of binary format. Items with the response format "almost every month, some months but not every month, or in only one or two months" were rescaled so that "almost every month plus some months but not every month" implied a degree of food insecurity, whereas "only one or two months" did not. Items with the response "often, sometimes, or never true" were likewise rescaled: "often" and "sometimes" implied a degree of food insecurity; "never" did not. This turned the eighteen items into a series of eighteen binary variables equivalent to eighteen yes/no questions. The USDA Food Security Scale is then the simple sum of the number of yes answers a particular respondent gives. So in households without children, the resulting scale can vary from zero (respondent provides food-insecure answers to *none* of the items) to ten (provides food-insecure answers to all ten of the questions asked of households without children); and by the same logic, in households with children under eighteen, the scale can vary from zero to eighteen.

Table 1.1 shows the distribution of the resulting scale for the 2013 administration of the Food Security Scale (Coleman-Jensen, Gregory, and Singh 2014). It also shows the "cut points" used by the USDA to define various degrees of food insecurity.

Several comments are again in order. First, any nonzero score reflects *some* degree of anxiety about food, so at the outer limit, two-thirds to three-quarters of the US population are food-secure and the remainder are not. But the USDA has a stricter standard. In its view, persons answering yes to none, one, or even two items from the scale can all be considered food-secure. (In some presentations, the food-secure were those answering yes to none of the items, and the "marginally" food-secure were those answering yes to one or two of them.) Childless households answering yes to three to five of the items are classified as having "low" food security, and those answering yes to six or more are considered having "very low" food insecurity (the category that until 2006 was described as "food insecure with hunger"). If households also have children and therefore eight additional opportunities to answer yes, the criterion for "low" is increased to three to seven yes responses, and "very low" is increased to eight or more yes responses. All scale scores greater than two are described in USDA reports as food-insecure.

Food insecurity is higher among households with children present (approximately 20 percent food-insecure) than among childless households (approximately 12 percent food-insecure). As we will see later, the most serious food-insecurity problems are faced by younger, low-income families with children—not, for example, by seniors.

Table 1.1   Percentage of US Households by Food-Security
Raw Score, 2013

Number of Conditions Reported	Percentage of Households	Food Status
Households with children: 18-item scale		
0	69.3	Food-secure
1	6.2	(80.5%)
2	5.0	
3	3.9	Low security
4	2.9	(13.7%)
5	2.7	
6	2.2	
7	2.0	
8	1.8	Very low security
9	1.1	(5.8%)
10	1.0	
11	0.6	
12	0.5	
13	0.2	
14	0.2	
15	0.1	
16	0.1	
17	0.1	
18	0.1	
Households without children: 10-item scale		
0	80.5	Food-secure
1	4.2	(88.0%)
2	3.3	
3	3.4	Low security
4	1.6	(6.4%)
5	1.4	
6	1.8	Very low security
7	1.5	(5.4%)
8	1.0	
9	0.4	
10	0.7	

Prevalence of Food Insecurity in the United States

Using the preceding definitions and conventions, and as of 2013, 85.7 percent of all US households were food-secure, so 14.3 percent qualified as food-insecure—about one household in seven. (More recent surveys show the same essential pattern.) The latter figure includes 8.7 percent who were scored as having "low" food security and 5.6 percent who qualified as having "very low" food security. If we refer to the 5.6 percent as "hungry," hunger is just about as common today as it was in 1968—meaning half a century of no progress in resolving severe food insecurities.

The cut points used by the USDA to define the various categories of food insecurity are arbitrary. They arose initially because the USDA deemed the scale by itself "too detailed" to be a useful measure (Andrews, Bickel, and Carlson 1998). The cut points were created as "conceptually meaningful sub-ranges of severity" (Carlson, Andrews, and Bickel 1999:513S). The main role of the categories is to provide a consistent basis for comparison, and this they do. Still, why must a household have three or more affirmative responses to be considered food-insecure? The USDA admits that the thresholds are conservative, and others worry that this results in an underestimation (Coleman-Jensen 2010). Some scholars, including the author of the Radimer/Cornell measures of hunger from which the USDA questions are derived, suggest that since no objective guideline exists, even one affirmative answer is indicative of food insecurity (Radimer, Olson, and Campbell 1990; Radimer et al. 1992; Kendall, Olson, and Frongillo 1995). Does the difference between two and three yes responses amount to a qualitative difference in well-being? How about the difference between five and six?

Two further observations. First, all items specify some monetary reason for food insecurity, but as we have already argued, people can be food-insecure for reasons other than economics. Taking these other factors into account would increase the amount of food insecurity. Second, all the items refer to "the last twelve months" and therefore tell us nothing about the *chronicity* of food insecurity. We know from studies of poverty that the number of the poor in any given year is fewer than the number poor at least once in five or ten or twenty years (Devine, Plunkett, and Wright 1992); the same is true of homelessness and most other social problems, and the same is presumably also true for food insecurity. Extending the timeframe of the questions to twenty-four or forty-eight or sixty months would also serve to drive up the numbers. There is, after all, nothing magical about "the last year."

One of our students interviewed senior citizens on the Orange County "Meals on Wheels" waiting list and found some serious discrepancies between the answers given to the USDA items and their qualitative dietary accounts. One respondent answered the third question—"I couldn't afford to eat balanced meals"—with "never," but when asked what she actually ate, it was instant oatmeal for breakfast, toast for lunch, and a baked potato for dinner, supplemented occasionally with a can of vegetables or pickings from a leftover holiday ham. Other respondents reported that they *always* ate balanced meals but mainly consumed cheese and crackers, canned peas and beans, frozen pizzas, cereal, and mashed potatoes. Many got by on snack items but reported them as "balanced meals" (Gualtieri and Donley 2016). Clearly, the USDA questions do not define terms such as "balanced meals," "run out," "skip meals," and so on, and as a result, different respondents interpret the question in different ways.

The USDA items also do not address the important issue of *adaptation* or of possible tradeoffs families might make among food, housing, transportation, medical expenses, and other costs. A low-income single mother who decided years ago that feeding the family was the top priority might report no food insecurity—she knows she can "make it work" because she always has. Instead, she worries about how to pay the rent, how to get the car repaired, school clothes for the kids, or that someone in the family has to see a doctor. It is not obvious that anxieties about the family food supply are more important or serious than anxieties about how to pay the rent or cover medical expenses.

Theorizing Food Insecurity

As a general principle, food insecurity must result either from the inability of the planet's arable land to produce sufficient food for its human population or from the inability of the planet's food distribution systems (governments, transportation systems, economic systems, etc.) to distribute food adequately. An essential point is that in today's world, food insecurity is mainly a *distribution problem* and not a production problem.

The planet's land surface amounts to 36.7 billion acres. Of that total, about half is potentially arable, so the amount of arable land is on the order of 10–15 billion acres. At present, about 7 billion acres are being used for agricultural production. Assuming a US diet and level of consumption, one acre of arable land supports one person for one year, so the current world population of about 7 billion is still comfortably within the feedable range. At the average food consumption of Italians, the feedable number would approximately double; at the average Indian level of consumption, it would increase by four. (For all the preceding points, see Bradford 2012.)

In short, the planet produces an ample supply of food. The World Food Summit in 1996 reported that the 5.8 billion people on the planet at that time had, on average, 15 percent more food per person than the population of 4 billion did twenty years before. Today, the amount of food available per person is higher still. It is significant that few if any twentieth- or twenty-first-century famines have resulted from insufficiencies in the food supply. Famine results when conflict, corruption, isolation, poverty, and genocide prevent the available food from reaching those in need. This point is absolutely essential to a proper understanding of the global food-security situation.

The various famines that visited the Horn of Africa in the late twentieth century are cases in point. (For a useful overview of famine history in this region, see Rice 2011.) There was serious drought in the region in 1984. The Ethiopian population was devastated while the nearby Somalian population was spared. Were Somali farmers just better at avoiding the effects of drought? No. The Ethiopians starved because the military government of the time was engaged in a brutal civil war and did not come to the rescue of its citizens. Ten years before, an even more serious drought struck several parts of Somalia, and again there was no mass starvation because the Somalian government moved quickly to mobilize the population and seek international aid, which was quickly forthcoming.

Cut to 1992 and the major Somali famine of that and the subsequent two years. The droughts of those years were no more serious than those of the 1970s and 1980s, but between 1992 and 1994, 300,000 Somalis starved to death. Why? The Somali state had collapsed in 1991 and the country was overrun by marauding gangs who looted farmers' harvests and slaughtered resisters. Warlords overran the affected regions and prevented international food aid from being delivered. Boatloads of grain rotted on the docks of

Mogadishu because of a conscious plan to weaken and conquer the Somali countryside. Geopolitics and armed militias, not drought or productive insufficiencies, were the factors responsible for these devastating famines.

In short, global agricultural productivity is more than adequate given the present and likely future world population. The more pressing question is how long these levels of productivity can be maintained given the extremely high external inputs required by modern agrarian technologies. The food supply is adequate, but is it sustainable? We return to this point later.

The preceding speaks to the food security of the global community, and at that level, food security is an issue of global geopolitics, civil war, ethnic strife, power grabs, and the explicit use of famine as a political tool by corrupt warlords, religious zealots, and indigenous elites. Food insecurity can also be seen as a property of nation-states, with national variations resulting from national and cultural differences in food preferences, agricultural traditions, and farming efficiencies and inefficiencies. But increasingly, attention has turned to food insecurity as a property of households and communities—of specific families, of course, but also of neighborhoods, census tracts, even whole political jurisdictions—not necessarily because community level variables are the cause of food insecurity but because the level of communities is where solutions can be found and implemented. Molly Anderson and John Cook (1999) describe the concept of community food security as "practice in need of theory"—a possible solution looking for a proper intellectual foundation. (On the more general topic of food justice and food insecurity at the level of communities, see Broad 2016.)

The Anderson and Cook account weaves together various contemporary strands of thinking about food, access, sustainability, grassroots activism, democratic political participation, and human-scale food production systems into a tapestry of community food security. Thus, "practitioners and advocates of community food security . . . envision food systems that are decentralized, environmentally-sound over a long time-frame, supportive of collective rather than only individual needs, effective in assuring equitable food access, and created by democratic decision-making" (1999: 141). Clearly, community food security overlaps with the alternative-food movement, urban agriculture, community gardening, and a wide range of related grassroots efforts to reform food production, distribution, and consumption. All of these issues are taken up in this book.

Even as the conceptualization of food insecurity has shifted toward individuals and families, there remains the background recognition that food availability must be connected to a system of food production and distribution. Thus, "the links between individuals or households and the larger community, the nation, and the international economy are widely acknowledged to contribute to food security" (Anderson and Cook 1999:142). The question raised in the literature on community food security is whether any meaningful or significant share of production and distribution can be localized—in other words, whether communities can become more food-sufficient than they presently are. Evidently, urbanization, culture, historical traditions, and many other factors impose limits on community food security as a food security strategy. So a key objective in most discussions on community food security is to reduce the overall level of consumption and make more efficient use of arable land, which in turn implies a shift away from meat-based diets. Thus, powerful cultural factors come into the discussion on community food security.

At least three streams of community and food activism coalesce in the movement around community food security, with the result that this type of food security means different things to different people. Indeed, "loose and shifting coalition" would be a more accurate characterization than "movement." First are the community nutritionists and nutrition educators who stress the importance of community factors in impeding or promoting food access. Their agenda is to change food preferences and eating habits, to encourage healthy eating, and to promote plant-based diets. A second group are the activists and environmentalists whose focus is typically on environmentally sound, sustainable food production. Democratic decisionmaking and grassroots activism are also important to this faction; they are leading advocates for inclusion and community participation. Also at the table are community development interests, anti-hunger and anti-poverty groups, and the immense network of emergency food providers, food bank operators, soup kitchen and food pantry directors, emergency shelter operators, and the like. The latter group is typically focused on equity in access to food. In embracing such a wide swath of community food activists and movements, community food security must struggle with competing agendas and issues.

To the extent that movements around community food security share common features, Anderson and Cook (1999:145) summarize them as follows:

- Multidisciplinary and systems approach to planning and implementing food security programs; thus, a formal recognition that no one discipline, approach, or constituency has the whole answer.
- Focus on whole communities rather than isolated sites.
- Broad community participation in issue identification, planning, needs assessment, formulation of interventions, and program implementation.
- Multisector linkages (i.e., coalition-building; inclusion of nonprofit organizations, businesses, and individuals from many different parts of the food system; a place at the table for all stakeholders).
- Emphasis on "farm-to-table" distribution, locally grown food, community gardens, farmers' markets, sustainable agriculture, and the like, in strong preference to "factory farming" and carbon-intensive distribution systems, whenever possible.
- Multiple objectives in every project, each of which should produce, distribute, or otherwise expand access to high-quality food while simultaneously creating jobs, developing community economy, promoting networking and development of social capital, and training residents in useful employment skills.
- Preference for and explicit inclusion of locally owned small businesses (versus large national and international corporations).
- Formation of food policy councils to address local policy issues.
- Emphasis on planning for the long term.

The last point deserves emphasis. When groups focusing on community food security (say, local food policy councils) convene, there is a recognition that nothing is going to change overnight. The world obviously depends upon industrial-scale farming and international systems of transportation to feed its population—that will remain true for centuries. At the heart of the matter are people's food preferences, and these too will change only over the long term. About 5 percent of the US population say they are vegetarians when asked in national surveys (a number that has stayed constant for at least the past ten years). Getting this figure to 10 percent or 15 percent would be a serious challenge; getting it up to half, nearly insurmountable. Thus, the explicit focus is on the long term.

In the short term, the cause is hopeless. And the problem with the long term, of course, is that one in seven American households is food-insecure *now.*

Ironically, community food security does not address the food security issue. It is about cultural change, not about feeding today's population. It is a utopian vision, not a concrete plan to reduce food insecurity on a scale of years or decades. The emphasis on locally grown food, for example, ignores the economic inefficiencies of these modes of production; the emphasis on grassroots activism and democratic decisionmaking forgets that leaders always emerge in any organized activity (this is Robert Michels's "iron law of oligarchy"); the advocacy for plant-based diets ignores the explicit food preferences of 95 percent of the US population.

Food as Economic "Entitlement"

Economists who have written on food insecurity owe a great debt to Nobel Prize–winner Amartya Sen's seminal 1981 book *Poverty and Famines: An Essay on Entitlement and Deprivation* and a follow-up chapter on "Food, Economics, and Entitlements" in his 1991 book coedited with Jean Drèze, *The Political Economy of Hunger.*

Sen's analysis begins with the observation that famine is less a problem of food production than a problem of who is and is not *entitled* to the food that is produced. Here, entitlement has a strict economic meaning and is not construed in the colloquial sense (i.e., in the sense that all people deserve some basic quantity of food). Economic entitlements to food are secured either through direct ownership of food (i.e., food producers, farmers) or through the conversion of wealth or income to food (everyone who does not directly produce food but must enter exchange markets to obtain it). As the world's agrarian (peasant) population has declined because of urbanization and increased agricultural productivity, those whose entitlements to food depend on their wages have increased. Famine, in this view, is a crisis in the entitlement to food, not usually a crisis of production.

Prior to Sen's analysis, economic studies of the world's food situation basically asked whether the world food supply was or was not growing faster than the population, reflecting obvious Malthusian influences. Political responses were largely confined to increasing food outputs. Sen's perspective called attention to the irony that, whereas global food production easily outpaced global population growth (in the 1980s and 1990s and even today), various regions of the world were wracked with widespread hunger and famine.

Cases in point were the Bengali famine of 1943, the Ethiopian famine of 1973, and the Bangladeshi famine of 1974 (Sen 1981). In these years and places of widespread starvation, food output had actually increased. The same was true of the various Horn of Africa famines discussed earlier. The 1969–1971 and 1980–1982 famines in the Sahel saw 5 percent declines in food production in Chad and Burkina Faso, a 7 percent decline in Senegal, a 12 percent decline in Niger, a 17 percent reduction in Mali, an 18 percent reduction in Ethiopia, and a 27 percent reduction in Mauritania. Millions starved in these famines. Yet, in the same years, there was a 5 percent decline in food production in Venezuela, a 15 percent decline in Egypt, a 24 percent decline in Algeria, a 27 percent decline in Portugal, a 29 percent reduction in Hong Kong, a 30 percent reduction in Jordan, and a 38 percent reduction in Trinidad and Tobago—but there was no famine in any of these nations.

Aside from factors of civil war, ethnic strife, and political corruption, a key difference in these examples is that the African nations of the Sahel relied primarily on food production as a means of obtaining income for exchange, whereas the economies of the other nations were more diversified. So when the agrarian sector collapsed, so did the entire economy. All forms of entitlement disappeared. In more diversified economies, food entitlements (aggregate incomes) were less drastically affected, and starvation was avoided.

Sen's essential contribution was to construe food insecurity as an issue of entitlement, or in a more common term, wages, and thus to render the issue as a poverty problem and an element of social stratification. The supply of food and the distribution of entitlements to food are not the same thing and, indeed, may be only loosely related. The implication is that a proper understanding of food insecurity must take wages, prices (of food and other essential commodities), and employment into account, not just the efficiency of the agrarian economy.

Sen's analysis has been influential in how advanced societies think about famine relief. A key implication is that cash is a reasonable alternative to food aid, a position that has been adopted by Oxfam and other international aid agencies. When the developed economies ship boatloads of food to famine-stricken areas, it stimulates government corruption and inefficiency on the receiving end, poses transportation issues in getting food into the stricken regions, and forces the population into relief camps where food can be distributed more effectively. Cash avoids these inefficiencies, prevents the movement of food out of the affected regions, and encourages employment and infrastructure investments by pushing more money into the local economy.

The parallel to food insecurity in the United States is intriguing. If food insecurity results from a lack of money (entitlement), the solution is to give food-insecure people more money. But here we confront a profound political and cultural issue, namely that we don't trust poor people with our money. So we have stumbled upon a deep theoretical link between Sen's analysis of global famine and the problem of food insecurity in the United States: cash may work better than food in both cases.

Indeed, the point generalizes. We have no issues depicting food insecurity in the less developed world as the result of politics, civil war, ethnic inequalities, and the like. But is the situation that much different in the advanced economies such as the United States? We will see in the next chapter that the strongest correlate of food insecurity is poverty. Poor people in the United States are cut off from the country's agricultural bounty no less than from all the other resources abundantly available to the middle class. Racial and ethnic correlates run along the predicted lines: whites thrive, while African Americans and Hispanics suffer. The major national effort of the United States to alleviate food insecurity among the lower classes is SNAP (Supplemental Nutrition Assistance Program), or food stamps, and conservative politicians at all levels have tried to gut the program at every opportunity and to demonize those who benefit from it. Since there is plenty of food to go around, how do we escape the conclusion that the US food insecurity problem also results from corrupt, self-satisfied, zealous, and indifferent elites?

An Anthropology of Resource Scarcity

An anthropology of food and water (resource) insecurity has been advanced by Amber Wutich and Alexandra Brewis (2014), focusing on three questions: What factors make communities vulnerable to resource scarcity? What strategies do households adopt to cope with resource insecurity? And what are the effects on individuals when their capacity to cope is overwhelmed?

There are about a billion people in the world who are chronically hungry and about a billion who lack access to safe, potable water, with considerable overlap between the two groups. Wutich and Brewis adduce three general propositions, each corresponding to one of the three theoretical questions that animated their research. First, defective institutional-scale factors make communities vulnerable to scarcity. The authors discuss five institutional factors that increase a community's vulnerability: basic ecology, population, governance, markets, and entitlements (the latter in the Amartya Sen sense). Ecology determines agricultural productivity; population sets the number of mouths to feed. These are described as necessary but insufficient conditions for resource scarcity. With respect to governance, "government policies can create food insecurity (e.g., agricultural or development policy) or fail to prevent it (e.g., food supplementation)" and are thus sufficient to "predict or explain some, but not all, community-level patterns of vulnerability to resource insecurity" (2014:447). Ditto for market factors such as hoarding, inflation, price increases, and market manipulation. Such factors sometimes explain all, sometimes much, and sometimes none of a community's vulnerability.

Following Sen, the interesting action in the institutional sphere is said to lie in entitlements—direct agricultural production, trade in resources, labor, wages and socioeconomic inequalities. The key insight here is that "scarcity is a problem of who gets a resource, not how much of it exists," in short, a problem of inequitable distribution, not insufficient production. "Entitlement failure may be sufficient to predict or explain many community-level patterns of vulnerability to resource insecurity" (2014:448).

Second, just as communities vary in their vulnerability to scarcity, so too do households vary in adaptive responses. Prior research suggests four key adaptive strategies: intensification, modified consumption, migration, and reprioritization or abandonment. Intensification means an intensified effort to obtain more food or water, such as by more labor-intensive farming of less productive lands (community gardens?), foraging (dumpster-diving?), increased efforts to generate income with which to buy food (panhandling?), or the sell-off of assets (pawnshops?). Our parenthetical comments acknowledge the potential relevance of these strategies even in the postindustrial economies.

Modified consumption is either eating less (cutting back on portion size or on the number of meals) or eating foods one would not normally consume. "Food-insecure households eat stigmatized or proscribed foods, sometimes called 'famine foods,' when preferred foods are unavailable" (2014:449). In contemporary advanced societies, this would include discarded food items (dumpster-diving) or, more generally, free-food programs: food stamps (SNAP), soup kitchens and congregate feeding programs, food pantries, Meals on Wheels, and the like.

Migration strategies include fostering out children, either temporarily or permanently, seasonal or temporary migration to more food-secure regions, or permanent resettlement. Intra-household reprioritization and abandonment are related strategies that involve denying resources to some to ensure that the needs of others are met (parents who go hungry so their children may eat), attending to the needs of some householders while ignoring others, or even abandoning the household's weakest members. These strategies alert us that resource scarcity may stimulate dysfunctional family dynamics, with negative effects on the family and its members.

Third and finally, individuals within resource-scarce households and communities vary in how they react to their situation. "Food insecurity is well-established as a trigger for rising levels of emotional distress and mental ill health, especially anxiety and depression" (2014:451). The intervening factors are uncertainties in the environment and stigma and shame within individuals. Perceptions of social injustice may also play a part. This hearkens back to the Maslovian theory that lower-order needs must be satisfied before consciousness is freed to pursue emotional well-being and other higher-order goals.

Conclusion

Seven key points have surfaced so far. First, food security and insecurity can be conceived as properties of specific individuals and households, of whole communities, of nation-states, or of the entire global food production and distribution system. The history of the concept has seen an evolution from broader to narrower conceptualizations, so most current research focuses on the food insecurities of individuals and families, a tradition followed throughout this book.

Second, despite half a century of pronouncements about ending hunger, the problem of food insecurity has proven obdurate even in affluent democracies. In the United States, the food-insecure proportion is in the vicinity of one in five to one in seven, and although these numbers are lower in places like Australia or Great Britain, no nation has been able to expunge food insecurity entirely.

Third, the food insecurity of people and households is now defined throughout the advanced English-speaking societies by a series of survey questions developed by the USDA. (In the developing world, different measures are needed.)

Fourth, judged locally, globally, or anywhere in-between, and with only rare exceptions, food insecurity is a problem of distribution, not of production. The planet produces plenty of food to go around, even at high levels of consumption. Periodic famines result from politics and the use of famine as a political instrument, not (usually) from crises of agricultural productivity.

Fifth, an economic analysis of food insecurity shows it to be an issue of food entitlements. In peasant and agrarian economies, entitlement is accumulated via direct production of foodstuffs, but for the vast bulk of the urban population, entitlement is accumulated via earnings and is indexed by income. In the United States, virtually everything the country does to address issues of food insecurity constitutes food aid rather than cash assistance (see Chapter 6). Is the US system of emergency food and food distribution the metaphorical equivalent of boatloads of grain rotting in the ports of Mogadishu? There is probably as much truth as simile in this comparison.

Sixth, in the United States and elsewhere, a principal response to food insecurity has been the movement around community food security. In Sen's terms, this movement can be analyzed as an effort to increase food entitlement via increased direct production of food. But while virtually any community could be reorganized to satisfy a larger share of its food needs, there are serious issues with this approach. Most food-insecure households will not be willing or able to grow the food they need.

Seventh and finally, communities and families vary in their susceptibility to resource scarcity, in their adaptive (or maladaptive) responses, and in how they are affected by their scarcity experiences. These points direct our attention to "modified consumption" and internal family dynamics as relevant household adaptations, and to the effects of food scarcity on the physical and emotional well-being of its victims.

Notes

1. All information on the early history of the USDA program is taken from https://www.ers.usda.gov/topics/food-nutrition-assistance/food-security-in-the-us/history-background.

2. In metropolitan areas, a food desert is a low-income census tract where at least a third of the residents live a mile or more from the nearest full-service supermarket; in nonmetro areas, ten miles or more. The USDA's Economic Research Service estimates that 23.5 million people live in food deserts, so the contribution of food deserts to the overall rate of food insecurity could be quite substantial.

3. While this book was in preparation, Wright was the director, Donley the associate director, and Strickhouser the project manager of the ISBS.

4. The novel was first published in 1962. The authorized English edition was published in 1991. The quotation appears at location 1946 in the Kindle version of the book.

2

The Correlates of
Food Insecurity

Scholars have studied issues of food insecurity for several decades, and a great deal is already known about the food-insecure population and how they adapt to their resource scarcity. Here we review the existing state of knowledge, relying on nationally representative data whenever possible but drawing on our own state and local studies to fill in important details.

In a recent national survey of food insecurity in the United States, 85.7 percent were food-secure by USDA standards and the remainder (14.3 percent) were food-insecure, with 8.7 percent qualifying as "low" in food security and 5.6 percent as "very low." These numbers have been mostly stable for several years—the problem is not dramatically worsening, but it is not getting better, either. How are the one in seven food-insecure Americans distributed across major social, economic, demographic, and geographical categories? Do food programs such as SNAP make any difference? Are their diets sufficient? Does food insecurity affect how people shop for food and prepare food? How do families cope? Finally, how does the food insecurity problem in the United States stack up against that in comparably advanced societies?

Income

Sen's analysis of food entitlement implies that food insecurity is a result of inadequate incomes, and indeed the strongest correlate of food insecurity is income (or poverty status): more income equates to more food security. This is true in every study ever done. Basic data are shown in Table 2.1.

Looking first at the total population, the data show a sharp and predictable gradient. At incomes under $10,000 annually, the food-insecurity rate hovers near 40 percent; from $10,000–20,000, about 30 percent; from $20,000–35,000, about 20 percent; from $35,000–50,000, near 10 percent; and above $50,000, less than 10 percent. The effect of poverty status is also as expected: above poverty, the food-insecurity rate is about 10 percent; below poverty, 35 percent. Similar findings are reported throughout the literature.

Clearly, food insecurity is largely but not entirely a poverty problem. To illustrate, in 2014 there were 41.7 million poor people in the

Table 2.1   Food Insecurity and Total Family Income, 2013

	Percentage Food-Insecure	
Income Category	Total Population	Households with Children
Under $5,000	34.3	43.6
$5,000–7,499	37.6	49.5
$7,500–9,999	38.6	48.9
$10,000–12,499	30.9	41.2
$12,500–14,999	28.0	38.9
$15,000–19,999	26.0	41.0
$20,000–24,999	21.7	36.3
$25,000–29,999	20.4	38.3
$30,000–34,999	17.6	31.7
$35,000–39,999	15.9	25.0
$40,000–49,999	11.0	16.6
$50,000–59,999	8.7	14.9
$60,000–74,999	6.6	10.7
$75,000–99,999	4.7	6.4
$100,000–149,999	2.8	3.3
$150,000 and up	1.4	1.7
Above poverty	9.9	12.4
At or below poverty	35.2	42.6

Source: 2013 Current Population Survey, Food Security Supplement, December.

United States (14.8 percent of the population). Among those, 35.5 percent were also food-insecure, which translates into 14.7 million food-insecure people in poverty. But there are 49 million food-insecure people in the United States. So although poverty is an important component, the majority of poor people (65 percent) are not food-insecure, and the large majority of food-insecure people (70 percent) are not below the poverty line. The relationship of food insecurity to income is strong, but not a perfect correlation.

How so many impoverished families manage to secure their food supply and therefore report little or no food insecurity is an important question, but the answer is likely obvious. Poor people who don't worry about food probably do worry about the rent, medical bills, and other expenses. All poor people, that is, probably have to worry about *something,* but just what that something is would vary from household to household.

The third column in Table 2.1 shows results for households with children, who have higher food insecurity at every level of income without exception. Among low-income households with children, the food insecurity rate hovers near 50 percent. As we will see later, the more children present in a household, the more severe food insecurity becomes.

A further indication that food insecurity is more than just a poverty issue is that there are at least some food-insecure families even at annual incomes of $75,000 and up—not many, but some. Mark Nord and Philip Brent consider whether this is just the result of erratic and unreliable response patterns to the USDA questions but conclude that it is not. "The study finds that a small proportion, at most, of measured food insecurity among middle- and high-income households appears to be due to misunderstanding of questions or to random or erratic responses. Some households in these income groups are food insecure due to factors such as uneven incomes or changes in household composition during the year or to the existence of multiple economic units in the same household" (2002:1).

Further analysis of this subgroup proves revealing. They are slightly younger on average than the sample as a whole, have larger families and more children, and are more educated than the general population. They are more likely to be African American compared to the total sample and appear to suffer from what could be labeled "underemployment" given their higher educations. Clearly, they are not destitute but seem unable to meet basic needs despite relatively high incomes. One possible explanation is that their incomes have allowed them to incur debt they are now struggling to honor—larger families, bigger houses, fancier cars, and other consumer goods bought on credit and now draining away income. They participate in food assistance programs much less frequently than the general population because they do not qualify for assistance at their income level. Yet almost half say they need to spend more on food and 86 percent acknowledge trying to make their food money go further.

Non-Economic Food Insecurity

The USDA conceives of food insecurity as a function of financial hardship, and given the strong relationship with income, that is appropriate. But some people can be food-insecure because there may not be a supermarket close to where they live; they may have transportation, mobility, or disability issues that interfere with access to food; or there may be cultural issues. What would happen to our estimate of the rate of food insecurity if these factors were taken into consideration? The rate would go up, but by how much?

At one time, our research group surveyed a sample of households in Orange County, Florida, and also a sample of Florida residents statewide. Because these were our surveys, we could ask questions that other surveys do not ask and thereby explore little-known topics. The Orange County survey, for example, contained three questions relevant to the issue of non-economic food insecurity, with results as shown in Table 2.2. The three questions ask about mobility or transportation issues ("no way to get to the store"), food deserts ("no grocery near to where you live"), and cultural preferences ("stores don't have the food items you and your family like to eat"). All of these are issues for at least a few respondents. One respondent in twenty, for example, has mobility issues getting to a grocery, about 2 percent profess not to have a grocery store anywhere near where they live, and another one in twenty ran short on food at least once last year because the places where they shopped didn't have the food they liked to eat. These are small numbers, but if these responses are added to the food-insecurity index, the estimated rate of food insecurity (for Orange County, Florida) would increase from 17.2 percent to 19.3 percent—a 12 percent increase over the baseline value. Phrased differently, if these Orlando-area results generalize, then about 10 percent of the total food-insecurity problem would result from non-economic factors. Whether national data would show similar results is unknown and will remain so until somebody adds these questions to a food-insecurity survey.

Further analysis showed, contrary to expectation, that mobility and transportation issues were spread evenly across the age spectrum. This was cited as an issue by 6 percent of those under age sixty and by 5.9 percent of those age sixty and over. Not having a nearby grocery was more problematic for low-income families than upper-income families. In the two lowest-income groups, this was cited as problematic by just over 5 percent; in the two highest-income groups, by barely 1 percent. Finally, many more Hispanics (8.2 percent) than non-Hispanics (3.7 percent) ran short on food because the stores where they shopped did not carry the food items they liked to eat.

Table 2.2   **Food Insecurity as a Result of Food Deserts, Mobility Limitations, and Cultural Preferences, 2014**

"Still thinking about the last 12 months,
did you or your family
ever run short on food because:

	Orange County	Orlando	Total
. . . you had no way to get to the grocery store?"			
% Yes	5.2	10.3	6.2
Of those, % "almost every month" or "some months"	63.2	68.4	64.9
. . . there is no grocery store near to where you live?"			
% Yes	2.1	3.4	2.3
Of those, % "almost every month" or "some months"	80.0	66.7	76.2
. . . the places where you shop just didn't have the food items you and your family like to eat?"			
% Yes	4.7	6.3	5.0
Of those, % "almost every month" or "some months"	50.0	54.6	51.1

Source: Orange County Survey.

Age

The usual assumption is that food insecurity increases with age, or at least that seniors are disproportionately food-insecure. To dramatize the problem of senior hunger, many public figures (e.g., Jesse Jackson and Florida congresswoman Frederica Wilson) have alleged that seniors are often reduced to eating pet food because that is all they can afford. Wilson said in 2013 that "senior citizens in my district eat dog food when their food stamps run out," and added, "I'm sure that somewhere in America today some poor soul is relying on dog food to take them through the month."[1] In 2012, politicos in Washington, D.C., took the meme to an even more absurd level. A Social Security proposal circulated late in the year arguing that if old poor people were eating cat food to save money, then Social Security recipients "should only be getting enough to pay for cat food."[2]

Nothing but anecdotal evidence has ever been presented to show that seniors resort to dog and cat food to meet their nutritional needs, and as a matter of fact, every available study concludes that the most food-insecure subgroup in the United States are young, low-income families with children, and that food insecurity tends to *decline* with age. Data are shown in Table 2.3.

In these data, the rate of food insecurity is highest among the youngest age category and declines steadily as age increases. Persons ages eighteen to thirty-four report three times more food insecurity than persons age seventy-five and older. Moreover, this is not a statistical fluke, as identical patterns have been reported in every study we examined. For all the attention given to senior hunger, there turns out to be more food insecurity among the young.

Yet if we do a Google search for "state programs that address senior hunger," we turn up dedicated "senior hunger" programs in at least half the states and in dozens of cities. Why all the fuss about senior hunger if they are more food-secure than other age groups?

There are many reasons why senior hunger has commanded an outsized share of attention. First, although food insecurity is less common among seniors, the consequences for seniors are generally more severe—often much more. We return to this point later. Moreover, seniors are often retired, immobile, and stricken with multiple chronic diseases and disabilities, so the usual advice to people experiencing economic hard times—get a job—simply does not apply. As the life cycle winds down, people deserve better.

Table 2.3   Food-Insecurity Rates by Age, 2013

Age	Secure	Insecure
18–34	81.6	18.4
35–49	83.9	16.1
50–59	84.8	15.2
60–64	87.0	13.0
65–69	89.4	10.6
70–74	92.6	7.4
75+	94.0	6.0

Source: 2013 Current Population Survey, Food Security Supplement, December.

As we reported elsewhere (Strickhouser, Wright, and Donley 2015), over 9.5 million seniors—17.3 percent—experience some form of food insecurity. If we exclude the marginally food-insecure, there are 5.5 million food-insecure seniors, of whom about 2.2 million are at risk of hunger. Although certain groups of seniors are at greater risk, senior hunger cuts across the income spectrum. Over half of the seniors at risk for hunger have incomes above the poverty line. Likewise, food insecurity is present in all demographic groups. Over two-thirds of seniors at risk of hunger are white. There are marked differences in the risk of hunger across family structure, especially for seniors living alone or caring for a grandchild. Those living alone are twice as likely to experience hunger compared to married seniors. One in five senior households with a grandchild (but no adult child) present is at risk of hunger compared to about one in twenty households without a grandchild present.

Seniors are also more likely to suffer from food insecurity if they are low-income, relatively young (sixty to sixty-four), high school dropouts, African American, Hispanic, renters, or lacking sufficient access to emotional and financial support. In a 2011 report, James Ziliak and Craig Gunderson found that food insecurity had increased significantly after 2007 across all groups of older adults. Food insecurity among seniors was highest in the South (Strickhouser, Wright, and Donley 2015). Predictions are that by 2025 an estimated 9.5 million elderly Americans will experience some form of food insecurity beyond "marginal," with about 4 million severely food-insecure.

A more interesting question is why older people are less food-insecure than younger people in the first place. One answer is the dynamics of the life cycle. Younger people are usually at the start of their careers, when pay and job security are lowest. As the years accumulate, compensation and job security increase. Then in one's sixties, certain age-related benefits become available: Social Security, Medicare, and senior discounts on nearly everything. Too, survey data reflect only the non-institutionalized population, and if food-insecure seniors are more likely to be institutionalized (almost certain to be the case), then the least-food-secure seniors would be removed from the data. Finally, it may be that the most-food-insecure seniors suffer higher than average mortality, and this too would tend to produce the pattern shown in Table 2.3.

Gender, Race, and Ethnicity

Men report less food insecurity (11.6 percent) than women (16.8 percent), but this mainly reflects the high rate of food insecurity reported by single women with children (29.5 percent). Among husband-wife households (with or without children), the male-female differences are insignificant (and the overall rate is under 10 percent). Differences by race and ethnicity are as would be expected. Whites report a food insecurity rate of 12.4 percent, while the rates are about twice that among blacks and Hispanics (25.9 percent for blacks, 23.6 percent for Hispanics). Interestingly, in a multivariate analysis[3] holding income and other factors constant, the Hispanic distinctiveness largely vanishes (odds ratio for being Hispanic = 1.06) whereas the black distinctiveness does not (odds ratio for being black = 1.37). So for Hispanics, income is the key factor, while for blacks, other factors predominate.

Household Composition, Marital Status, and Effects of Children

One of the surprising lessons of the University of Michigan's Panel Survey of Income Dynamics was that demographic factors such as family formation, dissolution, or family size had larger effects on annual income fluctuations than job loss or reductions in hours, and the same dynamics apparently affect levels of food insecurity. Basic data are in Table 2.4.

Table 2.4   Food-Insecurity Rates by Marital Status, Household
Composition, and Number of Children, 2013

	Secure	Insecure
Marital status of respondent		
Married	90.7	9.3
Widowed	88.8	11.2
Divorced/separated	76.9	23.1
Never married	80.6	19.4
Household type		
Intact husband-wife	91.9	8.1
Lone adult male with children	78.6	21.4
Lone adult female with children	70.5	29.5
Lone male without children	85.2	14.8
Lone female without children	84.9	15.1
Household size		
1	85.2	14.8
2	89.4	10.6
3	84.7	15.3
4	84.6	15.4
5	81.6	18.4
6	73.2	26.8
7+	69.0	31.0

Source: 2013 Current Population Survey, Food Security Supplement, December.

Married people are the least food-insecure (9.3 percent), and divorced and separated the most (at 23.1 percent). The widowed and never-married rates (11.2 percent and 19.4 percent, respectively) reproduce the effects of age: younger ages mean less food security; older ages mean more. The interesting result is the effect of marital dissolution, no doubt reflecting the effects of divorce and separation on poverty among women.

Household type shows largely the same patterns. Intact husband-wife households predictably show the lowest food insecurity, at 8.1 percent. Single parents raising children, whether male (rare) or female (not so rare), face elevated food-insecurity rates (21.4 percent and 29.5 percent respectively, with the single moms worse off). Among lone-male and lone-female one-person households, rates are effectively identical. So the gender difference noted earlier is almost entirely the result of the greater numbers of single moms over single dads.

Finally, total household size shows the predictable pattern: more mouths to feed implies less food security. Food insecurity among one-person households is slightly elevated relative to two-person households (14.8 percent versus 10.6 percent), reflecting the lower average age of the former group, but thereafter food insecurity increases regularly as household size increases, peaking at 31 percent for households of seven or more persons. The magnitude of the effect of household size rivals that of income.

Geography: Region and City Size

Traditionally, the highest rates of food insecurity are found in the Southern states and the lowest in the Northeastern states. Our data reproduce this pattern, although the differences by region are not large: 15.7 percent in the South; 12.3 percent in the Northeast, with the other regions in between. Nor does one find a sharp city-size gradient, with a metro versus nonmetro difference of about 2–3 percentage points (nonmetro areas have slightly higher rates). The expectation that the lowest rates would be found in suburban areas is not confirmed. Rates of food insecurity are largely flat across city sizes. There is solid evidence to believe that rates were lower in the suburbs prior to the 2008 recession but that the recession hit suburban families particularly hard so that the suburban distinctiveness was wiped out (Coleman-Jensen 2010). Today, if anything, the rates are slightly elevated in the suburban communities.

Our research group has been interviewing food pantry users throughout the Orlando metro region for years. Some of the pantries are in the highly urbanized central city, but many are located in the outlying suburbs. In Orlando at least (and possibly elsewhere), suburban food pantry users were largely female (61 percent), white (72 percent), non-Hispanic (59 percent), working (69 percent), and with no children in public schools (64 percent). Only about one in three received food stamps. Food services, health care, and employment services were the most frequently stated needs. Most (70 percent) visited their pantry weekly; about one in four said they also visited other food pantries from time to time. In response to a question about skipping meals "because you do not have enough food," 58 percent said they did not and the remainder did skip meals either regularly or from time to time. In all places where comparisons are possible, the suburban food pantry patrons looked much like patrons in the inner city except for their racial composition. There was no indication that the suburban patrons had less pressing needs or a less severe level of food insecurity.

The CBS Documentary Revisited

The overall level of food security has not improved since the CBS documentary "Hunger in America." Has the geographical distribution of food insecurity changed? Apparently not. There are substantial research literatures on food insecurity in all four of the geographies explored in the CBS original: Appalachia, the Mississippi Delta, Indian reservations, and the black inner city. Much of the research on food deserts, for example, has focused on poor urban black (and Hispanic) neighborhoods where access to food is problematic. All studies conclude that food insecurity is strongly related to race and income, so the food situation in the black inner cities has almost certainly not improved in the past several decades.

Several research groups explore food issues in Appalachia, for example, at North Carolina State and at the University of North Carolina at Wilmington. These groups routinely report on the high levels of food insecurity in the region (see, e.g., Pheley et al. 2002 or Hewage 2014).

Much the same is true of the Mississippi Delta. Levels of food insecurity, obesity, and physical inactivity remain high in the Delta in comparison to surrounding regions (Harrington et al. 2014); according to one study, "obesity, diabetes and hypertension have reached epidemic levels in the largely rural Lower Mississippi Delta" (Tussing-Humphreys et al. 2013:1), largely because of inadequate diets. Another study confirms that the food-insecure in the Delta eat a particularly low-quality diet (Champagne et al. 2007).

The original inhabitants of North America, people we erroneously call "Indians," are among the most impoverished subgroups of all, and the rates of food insecurity among Native Americans are high. Marla Pardilla and colleagues (2014) have documented high levels of household food insecurity on the Navajo Nation. Among a sample of 276 Navajos, 77 percent exhibited some degree of food insecurity, probably the highest food-insecurity rate ever registered for a population group in the United States. Elevated food insecurity has also been observed among Alaskan Inuits (Huet, Renata, and Egeland 2012) and among indigenous First Peoples in Canada (Genuis et al. 2015).

Food Insecurity and Program Participation

Why, given all the programs available to provide food to those in need, is there still a food-insecurity problem? Many people seem to think that existing public and private programs must adequately deal with hunger and food insecurity. SNAP enrollment now tops 46 million nationwide, by far the largest feeding program in the United States. The free and reduced school feeding programs serve 11 million mainly low-income children breakfast each school day and 22 million at lunch. Some millions more are served through the Women, Infants, and Children (WIC) program, and still more millions through Meals on Wheels. Then there are the tens of thousands of food pantries and soup kitchens where food-insecure people can obtain emergency food more or less on demand. With all these programs up and running, how can there be any serious food insecurity left?

The answer, of course, has to do with the accessibility of and participation in the various feeding programs. Consider SNAP. In the national data, overall participation in SNAP stands at 26.5 percent of the entire population. Among the food-insecure, the rate is 42.8 percent. So the good news is that the food-insecure are much more likely to be SNAP recipients. The bad news is that fewer than half of food-insecure people and families participate. Clearly, SNAP cannot eliminate food insecurity if half the food-insecure do not participate.

Table 2.5 shows the relationship between SNAP participation and food insecurity for the three lowest-income groups in our Orange County food-insecurity survey. (Again, we rely here on the Orange County data because we have not been able to locate national data that ask the same questions.) It is clearly *not* the case that being in SNAP ends food insecurity among low-income families. To the contrary, in all of our low-income groups, SNAP participants show higher levels of food insecurity than nonparticipants, by substantial margins. (This is also true in the statewide and national data.) In the lowest-income group, to illustrate, 64 percent of those who are not SNAP participants are nonetheless food-secure, versus only 45 percent of those who are SNAP participants.

This result is not necessarily unexpected. SNAP enrollment processes may well favor the most food-insecure families, such that those with the most serious problems are the most likely to receive help. All else equal, the fewer a family's resources, the lower its income, and the larger its size, the more likely it is to qualify for ben-

Table 2.5   Food Insecurity and SNAP Participation, 2014

	Income Category					
	Extremely Low		Very Low		Low	
SNAP participant	Yes	No	Yes	No	Yes	No
Food-secure (%)	45	64	52	63	62	81
Moderately food-insecure (%)	34	25	32	25	25	12
Very food-insecure (%)	21	11	16	13	12	7
Number of respondents	74	36	25	56	24	96

Source: Orange County Survey.

efits, and the larger that benefit will be. All of these factors also promote food insecurity. There are also special eligibility rules for elderly and disabled persons. With that in mind, the pattern shown in Table 2.5 may only reflect that, even within income categories, the most seriously resource-poor are those most likely to qualify for SNAP benefits. This is the optimistic explanation.

The pessimistic explanation is that SNAP increases people's insecurities about food. SNAP certifications expire (after twelve, twenty-four, or thirty-six months depending on an individual household's situation) and must be renewed with an application, new forms, and a new personal interview. A recipient family must locate a grocery outlet that accepts SNAP payment and be prepared to live with whatever stigma comes with using a SNAP or electronic benefit transfer (EBT) card. Rules governing what can and cannot be purchased under SNAP are a confusing morass of seemingly arbitrary guidelines insensitive to individual needs. Finally, the average monthly SNAP benefit, while better than nothing, may not be sufficient to put a serious dent in a participating family's food insecurity. In Florida in 2014, the average monthly SNAP benefit was $237, or less than $8 per day—barely enough to feed one person, much less a family.

SNAP, of course, is not the only feeding program available to families. Some will be eligible for home-delivered meals, some may participate in congregate feeding programs, and still others may make use of the food pantries. Survey data from the Orange County study on participation in these programs by level of food insecurity are shown in Table 2.6. The first two of these programs (Meals on Wheels and congregate feeding programs) are intended mainly for seniors and are not necessarily targeted to the food-insecure, although they are used primarily by food-insecure seniors. Usage of both programs increases as food insecurity increases. The equivalent questions in the national data show a participation rate in Meals on Wheels of 7.8 percent among the food-insecure and a rate of 9.0 percent among the same group for congregate feeding programs, somewhat higher but generally comparable to the Orange County results.

The Orange County survey asked, "In the last 12 months, did (you or other adults in your household) ever get emergency food from a church, a food pantry, or food bank?" In the total sample, 6.1 percent of 890 respondents said yes. Food pantry usage is heavily concentrated among the food-insecure. Nineteen percent of moderately food-insecure persons and 37 percent of severely food-insecure persons had obtained emergency food from a food pantry in the preceding twelve months. In the national data, 11.4 percent of the total population and 26 percent of the food-insecure population said that they "received food from a food pantry in the last twelve months," roughly the same results as in the Orange County survey. Evidently, the pantries are doing what they were intended to do—serve the food-insecure—but when only two in five severely food-insecure families and one in four of the food-insecure in general make use of the pantries, a great deal more outreach is required before participation will reach even half the population in need.

Whether users of the system or not, all respondents in the Orange County survey were asked, "To the best of your knowledge, is there a church, food pantry or food bank in your neighborhood where you

Table 2.6   Food Insecurity and Feeding-Program Participation, 2014

		Secure	Moderately Insecure	Severely Insecure
Free home-delivered meals?	% Yes	0.9	1.9	6.5
Any congregate meals?	% Yes	1.4	2.8	6.5
Use a food pantry?	% Yes	2.3	18.9	37.0
Know of a food pantry?	% Yes	52.7	49.1	56.5
Ever heard of 2-1-1?	% Yes	12.2	22.6	32.6
If Yes: Ever used 2-1-1?	% Yes	21.1	45.8	64.3

Source: Orange County Survey.

could get emergency food if you needed it?" In the total population, just over half (53 percent) said yes, there was; 17 percent said no, there was not; and 30 percent simply did not know. Awareness of a food outlet in the neighborhood was about the same in all categories of food insecurity.

A final question asked whether people in Orange County had ever heard of 2-1-1, the emergency services hotline operated by Heart of Florida United Way. (Similar 2-1-1 systems exist throughout the United States.) In the total sample, as in other surveys where questions about 2-1-1 have been asked, a relatively small minority of 14.5 percent said yes. Again, the good news is that awareness of 2-1-1 definitely increases with food insecurity; among the moderately food-insecure, 2-1-1 awareness rises to 23 percent, and among the severely food-insecure, to 33 percent. But this still leaves large majorities of those in need who have never heard of the 2-1-1 system.

In sum, available programs of assistance to the food-insecure may ameliorate the problem but certainly do not solve it. By far the largest program is SNAP, and low-income SNAP participants are no more food-secure than their nonparticipant counterparts and are possibly even less food-secure. Concerning food-insecure seniors specifically, national data show that income-eligible seniors are less likely to participate in SNAP than any other identifiable demographic. Other programs have even lower participation rates and therefore address even smaller slices of the overall need. The system of food pantries holds out perhaps the most hope of getting emergency food to those in need, and they are heavily utilized by needy families. And yet only about half of our Orange County respondents—the food-secure and food-insecure alike—are even aware of an emergency food outlet in their neighborhood. A key tool in the struggle against food insecurity at the community level must therefore be increased awareness of the available resources by people in need.

Food Insecurity and Coping Strategies

There are, of course, many things food-insecure families can do to cope. One important strategy is to make food the priority and worry about how to cover other expenses. An alternate strategy is to make food go further—reduce portion sizes, skip occasional meals, purchase less expensive food, and utilize pantries and community feeding programs. A single question in the national survey asks whether respondents do anything at all along these lines. In the general population, 24.1 percent said yes. Among the food-insecure, 87.1 percent said yes. So it is not as though the food-insecure are indifferent to the situation they face or unwilling to do what they can to address it.

A related question in the national survey asks where food had been purchased in the preceding week. Supermarkets were mentioned by 89.0 percent and 85.6 percent of the total and food-insecure populations respectively—a trivial and insignificant difference. Warehouse clubs and produce stands were mentioned by 33.4 percent and 31.4 percent—also a trivial difference. The only significant difference of note was restaurants, mentioned by 62.1 percent of the total population but by only 46.0 percent of the food-insecure. So another coping strategy used by many of the food-insecure is to avoid eating in restaurants and cook at home instead. Surprisingly, the total dollars spent on food in a typical week was $123 for the total population and $106 for the food-insecure—a smaller than expected difference. But among the food-insecure, 59.6 percent said they needed to spend *more* for food each week; in the general population, the figure was only 15.8 percent.

Other coping mechanisms not directly asked about in any of the surveys include food sharing among social networks (e.g., Tam, Findlay, and Kohen 2014) and borrowing or buying food on credit (e.g., Gupta et al. 2015). Most of these studies deal with less developed nations. A review essay on coping strategies among food-insecure people in the advanced societies (Chilton et al. 2013) lists such strategies as comparing oneself to others who are worse off; acceptance; denial; hunting and gardening; reducing dietary quality; using coupons and shopping for sales; dumpster-diving; finding a second or third job; participating in food assistance programs; using social networks; stealing food; putting children in foster care; and so on through a long, dismal list.

Food Insecurity and Disabilities

The national survey asks questions about six kinds of disabilities: deaf or hard of hearing; blind or difficulty seeing; difficulty remembering or making decisions; difficulty walking or climbing stairs; difficulty dressing or bathing; and difficulty doing errands. Persons suffering any one of the six disabilities have a 25.6 percent rate of food insecurity, well more than twice the rate in the total population. Among those who report their labor force status as "disabled," the rate is 40.7 percent. Percentaging in the other direction, among those who are food insecure, 18.2 percent list their employment status as disabled versus a mere 6.3 percent in the total adult population. Likewise, the food-insecure suffer all six of the asked-about disabilities at elevated rates (in most cases, about twice the rate for the total population). Controls for family income generally reduce but do not eliminate the effects of disabilities on food insecurity.

Chronicity of Food Insecurity

A common criticism of the USDA questions is that all of them ask about issues concerning access to food in the preceding twelve months and thus do not identify households who may be chronically food-insecure year after year. We know from other research that not all poor people are chronically poor and that not all homeless people are chronically homeless. Are all food-insecure people and households chronically food-insecure?

Three items from the Orange County survey (not asked in any other surveys we know about) were used to identify the chronically food insecure: "(I/We) worried whether (my/our) food would run out before (I/we) got money to buy more"; "The food that (I/we) bought just didn't last, and (I/we) didn't have money to get more"; and "(I/we) couldn't afford to eat balanced meals." In each case, respondents were first asked to state whether the statement was often true, sometimes true, or never true of themselves and their families in the preceding twelve months, and for those who said often or sometimes true, the follow-up asked, "How long has this been a problem for you and your family?" From the latter responses we infer the chronicity of their food insecurity. Basic results are in Table 2.7.

The pattern is very consistent. Somewhere between 18 percent and 22 percent of all respondents acknowledged that each of the three statements was often or at least sometimes true of themselves and their families; of those so acknowledging, about half indicated that this had been a problem for a year or less and the other half said more than a year. So by that measure, about half the food insecurity that exists (in Orange County and probably the nation as a whole) is chronic.

Table 2.7 Chronicity of Food Insecurity, 2014

	Often or Sometimes True (%)	Duration	
		A Year or Less (%)	More Than a Year (%)
Food would run out	22.4	47.7	52.3
Food didn't last	18.9	49.3	50.7
No balanced meals	17.8	38.2	61.8

Source: Orange County Survey.

The preceding treats each of the three items as a separate indicator, but if one sums across indicators for those who gave the "insecure" answer to any of the three indicators and then sums those who said at least one of these had been problematic for a year or more, the estimated chronicity rate rises to 63 percent. At the extremes, then, somewhere between 38 percent and 63 percent of the food-insecure are chronically food-insecure. "About half" seems a safe conclusion.

Similar findings are characteristic of other poverty-related conditions. For example, of all the women who receive welfare in any of ten consecutive years, about half are on welfare for two years or less. Likewise, in the span of a decade, about 36 percent of all families will be below poverty in at least one year while about a tenth will be below poverty in all ten years. Food insecurity appears to be a similar condition: around half is chronic, persisting over many years; the other half is episodic—occasionally problematic but not constantly so. And for obvious reasons, the more chronic condition will require different strategies of mitigation.

Or perhaps not. When we created a chronicity variable (equaling 1 if a food-insecure household said more than a year to any one of the three questions), the strongest zero-order correlates were household size, disability, and not owning a car. But in a multivariate binary logistic regression, *nothing* was significant in predicting chronicity. Thus, among the food-insecure, the chronics and the nonchronics are largely indistinguishable, leading us to the possibility that the important distinction is not between the chronics and others but between those who are already chronic and those on the way to becoming chronic, in which case the same interventions will be required for both groups.

Dietary Sufficiency

Food insecurity is a measure of uncertainty in the food supply. It does not in itself imply dietary insufficiency, only the possibility of food scarcities of various sorts. But data from items included in the Orange County study (and nowhere else, as far as we can tell) reveal a strong and important relationship between dietary insufficiency and food insecurity (see Table 2.8).

In the total county sample, nearly three-quarters reported an ample quantity and variety of food in the preceding twelve months; almost 80 percent said that they ate a nutritionally adequate diet all

Table 2.8   Dietary Insufficiency and Food Security, 2014

	Food-Secure	Food-Insecure
Generally speaking would you say that you and your family eat a nutritionally adequate diet . . .		
Enough of the kinds of food we want to eat	84.5	21.2
Enough but not always the kinds we want	13.8	41.0
Sometimes not enough to eat	1.5	26.3
Often not enough to eat	0.2	11.5
Number of respondents	748	156
Generally speaking would you say that you and your family eat a nutritionally adequate diet . . .		
All of the time	37.3	4.3
Most of the time	48.7	42.8
Sometimes	12.6	42.0
Rarely, Never	1.5	10.9
Number of respondents	684	138
And in terms of the quantity of food you eat, would you say that you and your family get enough to eat, not enough to eat, or too much to eat?		
Too much	15.9	6.4
Enough	82.8	74.2
Not enough	1.3	19.3
Number of respondents	685	140
Do you think you eat enough fruits and vegetables or do you think you should eat more?		
Eat enough	55.0	32.2
Should eat more	45.0	67.8
Number of respondents	737	151

Source: Orange County Survey.

or most of the time; 95 percent said their families had enough (or even too much) to eat; and just about half thought they ate enough fruits and vegetables. All of these numbers were dramatically worse for the food-insecure, among whom only 21 percent reported an ample quantity and variety of food; fewer than half said they ate a nutritionally adequate diet all or most of the time; about one in five said they did not get enough to eat; and two-thirds thought they should eat more fruits and vegetables. These are large differences and they underscore the very real problems food-insecure families have with access to food. The food-insecure may not be on the verge of starvation, and may not even be "hungry," but many do not have enough to eat and are unable to feed themselves a nutritionally adequate diet. Food insecurity is strongly related to suboptimal dietary intake.

In the total sample, 434 respondents agreed that they should eat more fruits and vegetables, and all of them were asked why they didn't. Topping the list at 32 percent was "they cost too much," followed by "they spoil too easily" (30 percent), "I just don't like them" (28 percent), "they take too much time to prepare" (19 percent), "I am not sure how to prepare or cook them" (9 percent), and "they are not available where I shop" (6 percent). Among low-income households, price and spoilage were even more prominent as reasons. A key point here is that cost is a far more serious issue than availability.

Similar items were included in our statewide survey. Overall, just under half (45.4 percent) of all respondents believed that they should eat more fresh fruits and vegetables. With respect to income, about half of low- and moderate-income respondents and over a third of high-income respondents believed they should eat more fresh produce. Here, too, those stating they should eat more were asked why they didn't. For low-income respondents, the most salient factor was again cost, with over half (53.4 percent) stating that fresh fruits and vegetables were too expensive. For the moderate- and high-income groups, the main reason given for not eating more fruits and vegetables was that they spoiled too easily.

A further measure of dietary insufficiency is the body mass index (BMI), scores for which are calculated from respondents' height and weight. By convention, BMI scores are recoded into categories of underweight, normal weight, overweight, and obese, according to national standards promulgated by the National Institutes of Health. Table 2.9 shows the results of these calculations across food-insecurity categories for the Orange County sample.

Table 2.9 Food Insecurity and Weight, 2014

	Number of Respondents	Percentage Overweight or Obese	Percentage Obese Only
Food-secure	715	61.7	25.3
Moderately food-insecure	102	70.6	34.3
Severely food-insecure	44	79.5	45.5
Total sample	861	63.6	27.4

Source: Orange County Survey.

In the total sample, about 64 percent are scaled as overweight or obese (27 percent are obese, 37 percent are overweight). In absolute terms, this may seem to indicate a county full of overweight people, but the Orange County rates are slightly below national norms. In the United States as a whole, 33 percent are overweight and 36 percent are obese, for a combined 69 percent (Flegal et al. 2012). Note also that the percentage of overweight and obese is lowest among the food-secure and increases as food insecurity increases. Among the severely food-insecure, nearly 80 percent are overweight and almost half (46 percent) qualify as obese by BMI standards.

A skeptic might look at these results and conclude that maybe the food-insecure are not so food-insecure after all. Clearly, they manage to obtain enough food to make themselves overweight at higher than average rates. But healthy food is expensive food, and cheap foods tend to be high in fat and carbohydrates and relatively low in protein and other nutrients. A steady diet of macaroni and cheese is fattening but not healthy; a steady diet of lean meats and fish with plenty of fresh fruits and vegetables is healthy, not fattening, but beyond the means of many food-insecure families. Eating well often costs more money than low-income families can afford to spend. We will come back to this point later.

How Does the United States Measure Up to the Rest of the Industrialized World?

Since there is no universally agreed-upon definition of "food insecurity," and since the very concept would have starkly different meanings in different social and cultural contexts, it is not surprising that strictly comparable data are available only for the advanced English-speaking democracies, specifically Canada and Australia. It is not that nations in Europe, Asia, Africa, and South America have no concerns about hunger or food insecurity in their countries. A quick Google search turns up multiple sources for many countries. The Middle Eastern and African nations have notably large literatures on the topic. But none of these research materials are derived from the standard USDA Food Security Scale or anything comparable.

The Canadians and Australians, however, have deployed measures highly similar to the Food Security Scale to document the extent and correlates of food insecurity in their countries. The most recent such study in Canada (that we have located) is titled *Income-Related Household Food Security in Canada,* published in 2007 by the Canadian Office of Nutrition Policy and Promotion. This report "provides, for the first time, national and provincial estimates of income-related food security at the household, adult and child level based on a standard multiple indicator measure of food security." This "standard multiple indicator measure" is the eighteen-item USDA Food Security Scale, used verbatim and scaled identically to how the USDA measure is scaled. This is as close to exact comparability as it gets.

One interesting departure from US practice is that the Canadians define a food-insecure person as anyone giving a yes answer to more than one item (versus the US standard of two). The report comments: "research has suggested that the food insecurity threshold of 'three or more' in the U.S. standard method may be overly stringent." But the summary tables show the results using both the more conservative US method and the less conservative Canadian method anyway.

By the US standard, 92.7 percent of all Canadian households qualify as food-secure; the equivalent US figure is 85.7 percent. The difference is one out of seven US households versus one out of twelve Canadian households, hardly a trivial difference. Staying with the US standard, the Canadian rate of moderate food insecurity is 4.5 percent (versus 8.7 percent in the United States) and the rate of severe food insecurity is 2.8 percent (versus 5.6 percent in the United States). Similar US-Canadian differences are found among households with and without children. Two conclusions follow. First, some degree of food insecurity is probably inevitable even in the most advanced and most affluent societies. But second, if the Canadians can get their food-insecurity rate beneath one household in ten, surely the United States can do likewise.

As in the United States, food insecurity in Canada is highest in single-parent households, households with young children, and households with three or more children of any age. There is also a strong relationship concerning family income, one that mirrors the US results. In the lowest-income category, for example, 48 percent of Canadians are food-insecure; in the highest, 1.3 percent. Interestingly, no table of data is presented showing food-insecurity rates by age for Canada.

The Australian data are not as comparable, but a questionnaire similar to the Food Security Scale showed a food-insecurity rate in Australia of only 5 percent (Rosier 2011). Again, family income was the strongest predictor. The Australian report also stresses the transportation angle. Households with no access to a car report sharply higher levels of food insecurity, just as in the United States. Food insecurity in Australia is highest among the young and declines with age; it is higher among single-parent and larger families, and also higher among people who are disabled, unwell, or frail. With a great deal of remote territory in the country, food deserts are also part of the problem.

In sum, where comparisons are possible, the correlates of food insecurity are essentially the same everywhere, but in the three nations discussed here, the prevalence of the problem is higher in the United States than elsewhere. Compared to the Australian one in twenty or the Canadian one in twelve, the US one in seven is embarrassing.

Notes

1. As reported by CNS News, July 15, 2013, https://www.cnsnews.com/news/article/congresswoman-some-my-constituents-eat-dog-food-when-their-food-stamps-run-out.

2. See http://ourfuture.org/20121214/dc-elites-literally-propose-old-people-eat-cat-food.

3. Our text refers to "multivariate analyses," multiple-regression analysis, and related statistical concepts at several points. We have not burdened the reader with the statistical details. If readers need access to those details, please consult the citations provided in the text. For a generally accessible introduction to multivariate analysis of social science data, see Hutcheson and Sofroniou 1999.

3

How Food Insecurity Matters for Mental and Physical Health

This chapter discusses various physical and mental health problems associated with food insecurity and what might be done about them. Health issues to be discussed include physical disability, increased stress or depression, poor management of chronic illness, increased hospital visits, and various other problems that contribute to or result from inadequate diets. In general, physical health issues associated with food insecurity have been more extensively studied than mental health issues, so our discussion of the mental health effects is sketchier than we would like.

The linkages between nutrition and health status are numerous, well-documented, and largely obvious. Inadequate diets are responsible for many physical disorders ranging from obesity to heart disease to increased susceptibility to infection. Since the food-insecure are least likely to consume a nutritionally sufficient diet, it follows that they would also be most likely to suffer from nutrition-related physical disorders. This chapter reviews and comments on the large number of studies that support this deduction.

It seems self-evident that all people should have routine access to a sufficient quantity and variety of food and that no one in a society as affluent as the United States should have to worry about where their next meal will come from. But what if they do? So what if people are uncertain from time to time whether they will have enough to eat later in the week? So what if they must occasionally skip a meal? Rates of obesity alone make it clear that many people could do with skipping some meals from time to time, so what's the big deal? This chapter is our effort to explain what the big deal is.

Food Insecurity and Obesity

It has been observed in numerous studies that food-insecure people are more likely to be overweight or obese (although some studies report a U-shaped rather than linear relationship—that is, that obesity is most common among both the highly food-secure and the highly food-insecure, and lowest otherwise). A review of fourteen studies by Lauren Dinour, Dara Bergen, and Ming-Chin Yeh (2007) concluded that the link between food insecurity and obesity was apparent in all population subgroups except nonelderly men. Brandi Franklin and colleagues (2012) reviewed nineteen studies conducted since the Dinour, Bergen, and Yeh paper; these studies "confirmed that food insecurity and obesity continue to be strongly and positively associated" (p. 253), particularly among women. More specifically, "food insecurity–obesity links among women remained consistent, with growing evidence among adolescents, mixed evidence among children, and sparse evidence among men" (p. 262). The basic relationship is now sufficiently well-established that it has been given a name: the "food insecurity–obesity paradox" (e.g., Dinour, Bergen, and Yeh 2007).

The interesting question, then, is not whether food insecurity is related to obesity but rather why this relationship exists. Numerous studies show that low-income, single-female-headed households, minority race, lower education levels, and larger families are all associated with food insecurity, and that each of these may be independently associated with obesity (Franklin et al. 2012; see also Drewnowski 2009). Some sort of multivariate analysis is necessary to determine what fraction of the overall effect is due to these intervening factors and what part is due to being food-insecure. As a general conclusion, statistical controls for these associated demographic factors usually reduce but do not eliminate the food-insecurity effect.

Parke Wilde and Christine Ranney (2000) (see also Kempson et al. 2002) explain the relationship between food insecurity and obesity with a proposed "food acquisition cycle." When food-insecure individuals have access to plentiful food (i.e., when food stamps or money is available), they overeat. This is followed by a period of involuntary food restriction (i.e., when waiting for new food stamps or money for food to become available) and followed again by overeating. (Studies show that on average, SNAP recipients use up about 80 percent of the total benefit in the first half of the month; see US Department of Agriculture 2011.) Kathryn Kempson and colleagues (2002) note that when food did become available to the food-insecure, they "ate as much as possible." According to one of the nutrition educators surveyed in this study: "They say stuff like, 'I have to store up as much as I can, because I don't know when I'm going to have the next meal'" (p. 1797). When food is made available to the food-insecure, overeating is a common response. Binge eating when food is plentiful followed by fasting when food supplies run dry, followed by more binge eating, results in excessive weight gain. Thus, compounding the irony, many food-insecure people are overweight not because they have access to too much food, but rather too little.

Many studies showing the effect of food insecurity on weight posit some version of the Wilde-Ranney "food acquisition cycle" theory to explain this relationship (e.g., Jones and Frongillo 2006; Dinour, Bergen, and Yeh 2007; Kim and Frongillo 2007; Webb et al. 2008; Pan et al. 2012). "Obesity may result from an adaptive physiological response to episodic food insecurity, which can lead to binge eating habits when food is plentiful. Cyclical food restriction has been associated with an increase in body fat, decrease in lean muscle mass, and a quicker weight gain with response to re-feeding" (Dinour, Bergen, and Yeh 2007:1958).

Eating a healthy diet is an expensive proposition, often costing more money than low-income families can afford. Other explanations link weight increases to the increased depression that often accompanies food insecurity, life experiences of particular cohorts, and uninhibited eating as a means of coping with certain stressors associated with food insecurity (Kim and Frongillo 2007; Ziliak and Gunderson 2011).

A study by Jennifer Mello and colleagues (2010) documents the linkages between food insecurity and dietary behaviors. With statistical controls for potential confounds (gender, age, ethnicity, marital status, income, education, employment status, household composition, and language spoken at home), the food-insecure consumed more fruit (but mostly in the form of fruit juice, so this was "not an entirely positive finding"), consumed more fat, and avoided fat-reducing cooking and eating strategies (broiling or baking instead of frying; draining grease from cooked meats). Other studies (Kendall, Olson, and Frongillo 1996; Frongillo et al. 1997; Tarasuk 2001) show that food-insecure people eat less fresh produce than do the food-secure. That the diets of the low-income population are suboptimal is commonplace in the nutrition literature.

Food insecurity is linked to obesity in almost all population subgroups with the exception of nonsenior men. Among seniors, the linkage is fairly strong. In a study of members of senior centers in Georgia (Brewer et al. 2010), food insecurity was not significantly associated with BMI measures of obesity after controlling for physical limitation but was significantly associated with waist circumference (WC) obesity. Weight-related disability was also significantly associated with food insecurity among seniors. The basic results have been replicated in numerous studies.

Food Insecurity and Self-Rated Physical Health Status

Aside from indirect effects of increased obesity on things such as Type 2 diabetes mellitus, gallbladder disease, coronary heart disease, high blood cholesterol level, high blood pressure, and osteoarthritis, food insecurity is directly linked to numerous negative physical health outcomes, including self-rated physical health status. Janice Stuff and colleagues (2004) conducted a survey of 1,488 randomly chosen adults living in the Lower Mississippi Delta. Food insecurity was identified using the standard eighteen-item USDA Food Security Scale. Self-assessed physical health status was measured with an abbreviated twelve-item version and two subscales. Controls for income, age, and ethnicity were applied to all statistical models. Results showed that food insecurity was associated with poorer self-rated general health status and lower scores on both physical and mental health subscales. "While we are not able to establish a causal relationship . . . there are a number of plausible biological mechanisms whereby food insecurity and poor nutrition lead to poor health. Malnutrition exacerbates disease, increases disability, decreases resistance to infection, and extends hospital stays. Other reports suggest that stress and anxiety (which may accompany food insecurity) induce high blood pressure and produce hormonal imbalances, and these together with additional factors can stimulate weight gain, obesity, and insulin insensitivity" (Stuff et al. 2004:335).

Health status is sometimes thought to be a function of access to and utilization of the health care system. And yet "psychosocial factors are among the most likely explanations for the disparities in health among different socioeconomic level groups. The stresses of economic insecurity may negatively affect wellness and induce individuals to make unhealthy lifestyle choices" (Bien et al. 2004:1). And of the nonhealth factors implicated in well-being, two of the most significant are nutrition and food security. "While it has long been known that a balanced diet contributes positively to health status, what has not been investigated until recently is the effect of an individual's surrounding environment upon nutrition and food security. Studies have demonstrated that societal and environmental factors have an influence upon food patterns and may pose serious risks to health" (Bien et al. 2004:2). These authors stress that proper nutrition encompasses much more than personal food preferences; it refers to "the social, economic, and cultural issues related to making the right food choices and to purchasing and eating the 'correct' types of food in the 'appropriate' quantities, as well as the factors that determine this aspect of essential daily human activity and behavior" (Shetty 2002:149).

Globally, the correlation between food insecurity and decreased physical health is almost universally accepted, as demonstrated through case studies linking food insecurity to "higher rates of HIV/AIDS, tuberculosis, anemia, micronutrient deficiencies, increased child and maternal mortality, stunted growth, underdevelopment of vital organs, and the prevalence of chronic diseases" (Hook 2015:1). Not all of these associations have been reported in data from the more advanced industrial societies, but many of them have. Without much doubt, food insecurity erodes physical well-being almost everywhere it is found.

Diabetes Mellitus

Fundamentally, diabetes is an error in the body's carbohydrate metabolism, and so we would expect people whose diet consists disproportionately of refined and processed carbohydrates to have a difficult time managing their diabetes. If you are food-insecure and diabetic, proper control of your diabetes proves to be quite a challenge. A 2014 paper by Enza Gucciardi and colleagues published in the journal *Current Nutrition Reports* reviews the pertinent literature. This review covers some thirty-nine research articles on various aspects of the linkages between food insecurity and diabetes. This substantial empirical research base supports several conclusions.

Food insecurity is more prevalent in households of diabetics than in other households, both in the United States and in Canada. Likewise, food-insecure households have a higher prevalence of diabetes than do food-secure households. Controls for potential confounds do not erase the relationship. Data from the National Health and Nutrition Examination Surveys (NHANES) show that "diabetes risk was approximately 50% higher among adults in food-insecure households than in food-secure households" (Gucciardi et al. 2014:326; see also Seligman et al. 2010). The elevated diabetes risk for the food-insecure remains in the face of controls for income, employment, physical health status, and various lifestyle factors, including obesity. The physiological linkage is that "diets common in food-insecure households (e.g., inexpensive carbohydrates) may increase dietary glycemic load, and therefore, increase the risk of diabetes" (Gucciardi et al. 2014:326).

Food-insecure individuals with diabetes face multiple challenges in food purchasing, meal planning, and food preparation. Some people with diabetes cope with these challenges by skipping meals, reducing portion sizes, and eating expired food. "People living with food insecurity often have limited control over their living environments, which can affect their ability to access and prepare healthy food" (Gucciardi et al. 2014:326). Foods available from retail outlets in low-income neighborhoods may often be limited to low-nutrition, relatively high-cost foods. Food banks, pantries, and soup kitchens offer little relief, since the food available in these outlets is often unsuitable for diabetics (too high in sugar, salt, and starch).

Diabetes management is also problematic. It has been widely reported that food-insecure people are more likely to doubt their ability to self-manage their diabetes. Proper diabetes management is itself an expensive proposition (requiring a glucometer, test strips, batteries, insulin, syringes, and more). Resource-challenged people such as the food-insecure often make tradeoffs between, say, buying supplies, buying medication, purchasing healthy food, or paying the rent. "Many forego medication to afford food. But more than a third of diabetics who visit food banks or soup kitchens pay for medication before food" (Gucciardi et al. 2014:326). Medication without food leads to insulin reactions; food without medication leads to hyperglycemia. The clinical effects of these tradeoffs are well-described in the literature (more hospitalizations for diabetes-related causes, more emergency room visits, more diabetes-related morbidity, and premature death).

Food-insecure people with diabetes consume less fruits, vegetables, and protein and more energy-dense foods than do their food-secure counterparts. Uncertainties in the supply of healthy food coupled with uncertainties about medication regimens lead food-insecure diabetics to poorer glycemic control, higher levels of glucose-containing hemoglobin, more hypoglycemic episodes, poor renal outcomes, more cardiovascular disease, and more overall morbidity. These patterns do not change under statistical controls for various confounds.

Food-insecure diabetics also report more physician encounters, more hospitalizations, and more emergency room visits than their food-secure peers. Food-insecure diabetics are also substantially more likely to miss checking their blood sugar levels (69 percent, compared to 13 percent), check their blood sugar levels less frequently due to inability to afford supplies (33 percent compared to 9 percent), often miss taking diabetes medications (33 percent compared to 18 percent), and take less medicine (or less often) than prescribed because they can't afford medication (39 percent compared to 14 percent) (Seligman et al. 2010; Seligman et al. 2011). Moreover, food-insecure diabetics are aware that these behaviors might drastically affect their diabetes but do not see that they have any choice (Biros, Hoffman, and Resch 2005; Seligman et al. 2010).

The prevalence of Type 2 diabetes increases with age, so all the effects just discussed are amplified among food-insecure seniors. Seth Berkowitz, Hilary Seligman, and Niteesh Choudhry (2014) found that even after controlling for clinical comorbidities, insurance, and demographic factors, cost-related medication under-use was more common in elderly respondents with food insecurity than among those who were food-secure (about 56 percent compared to 16 percent). In this study, cost-related medication under-use included being unable to afford a prescription, delaying a prescription due to cost, skipping doses due to cost, and taking less medication than prescribed due to cost. More than 11 percent of their sample, representing about 3.4 million Americans, reported both cost-related medication underuse and food insecurity.

Finally, food insecurity threatens the mental health of diabetics as much as their physical health. "Food insecure adults with diabetes are more likely than food secure adults with diabetes to report fair to poor overall health, mental health, satisfaction with life, and self-perceived stress" (Berkowitz, Seligman, and Choudhry 2014:327–328). Depression is also more common, as are anxiety, shame, powerlessness, and mood disorder. Diabetes is a major life frustration and even more so in the presence of uncertainty about food.

Food Insecurity and Mental Well-Being of Children and Adolescents

Stress corrodes mental well-being, and few things are more stressful than being uncertain whether you will have something to eat. Again, the expectation is that the food-insecure will score lower on any measure of mental wellness than the food-secure. Numerous studies show the linkage between food insecurity, self-rated mental wellness, and various indicators of psychological disease, although most of these studies focus on adults, not children or adolescents. A particularly large and well-done recent study of food insecurity and mental disorders among US adolescents (McLaughlin et al. 2012) is based on 6,483 thirteen- to seventeen-year-olds surveyed in the National Comorbidity Survey Replication, Adolescent Supplement, which was conducted from 2001 to 2004. Each child's parent or guardian was also interviewed about their child's mental health and developmental history.

Mental well-being was assessed with a modified version of the Composite International Diagnostic Interview (CIDI). CIDI-assessed disorders were grouped into four broad classes: mood disorders (depression, dysthymia); anxiety disorders (phobias, posttraumatic stress disorder [PTSD]); behavioral disorders (attention deficit hyperactivity disorder [ADHD], conduct disorders); and alcohol, drug, and other substance abuse. Food insecurity was measured with the USDA short-form Food Security Scale. Numerous indicators of family and community socioeconomic status were treated as covariates to ensure that effects of socioeconomic status were not being misinterpreted as the effects of food insecurity. Results showed, as expected, that food insecurity was relatively rare; food insecurity was strongly related to all measures of socioeconomic status (higher status equals higher food security); socioeconomic status is also associated with mental well-being (higher status equals higher mental wellness); and the effect of food insecurity on mental well-being is also strong and remains strong even once controls for socioeconomic status are introduced.

These results confirm that food insecurity erodes the mental well-being of adolescents but do not answer why. Katie McLaughlin and her colleagues speculate on two classes of intervening causal mechanisms. The first focuses on parenting quality. "Food insecurity likely represents a source of chronic stress for parents trying to provide basic necessities for their children and has been associated with parental mental health problems, including depression. Food insecurity therefore may influence child mental health through pathways related to parenting quality. Indeed, evidence has suggested that food insecurity is associated with less sensitive and responsive parenting" (2012:1300). A more physiological interpretation is that low caloric intake disrupts the hypothalamic-pituitary-adrenal (HPA) axis; HPA axis deregulation in turn "has been implicated in the pathophysiology of numerous youth mental disorders" (p. 1300).

What is true of adolescents seems also to be true of younger children, although the available research is sparse here, too. Robert Whitaker, Shannon Phillips, and Sean Orzol (2006) studied 2,870 mothers of three-year-olds in eighteen large US cities. These authors found that even controlling for socio-demographic factors, maternal physical health, alcohol use, drug use, prenatal smoking, and prenatal physical domestic violence, the percentage of mothers with either major depressive episodes or generalized anxiety disorders increased as food insecurity increased, and so did the percentage of children with behavioral problems. Other studies link food insecurity to children's behavior problems (Huang and Vaughn 2015), as well as disrupted sleep (Ding et al. 2015), lesser physical activity (To et al. 2014), school absenteeism and stunting (Bernal et al. 2014), poor dietary quality (Hanson and Connor 2014), and depression (Chilton et al. 2013).

Food Insecurity and the Mental Well-Being of Seniors

Food insecurity is associated with lower scores on both physical and mental health self-assessment scales among seniors, as well.

Assessments of mental health and depression used in these studies include the short-form twelve-item Health Survey, the Geriatric Depression Scale, and the eight-item version of the Center for Epidemiologic Studies–Depression (CES-D) Scale. According to these assessments, seniors who are food-insecure report more depression, decreased happiness and enjoyment of life, increased feelings of loneliness and sadness, and decreased effort and motivation to do things. In particular, the stressors associated with low socioeconomic status and disability (both of which lead to food insecurity) are known catalysts for the onset of depressive symptoms. These assessments have also shown that, among the elderly, women who report financial difficulty acquiring food are at greater risk for symptoms of depression than those who do not report such difficulty. This is particularly true among nonwhite senior women who are food-insecure (Klesges et al. 2001; Stuff et al. 2004; Kim and Frongillo 2007).

Food, Nutrition, and Senior Well-Being

Food insecurity is clearly not healthy for anyone. Much of the concern about senior hunger derives from the sense that proper nutrition is especially important in older people (e.g., Wells and Dumbrell 2006). As the American actress Bette Davis once observed, "Growing old is no place for sissies." The body and its nutrient requirements change throughout the life cycle and these changes accelerate in older ages. As people age, it becomes more difficult to distinguish between malnutrition and normal aging processes.

All of our senses become less acute as we age. Since we eat with our eyes and our noses as well as our mouths, when the acuity of smell, sight, and taste declines, food becomes less appealing and this too interferes with proper nutrient intake. The senses of taste and smell are not the only significant gastrointestinal (GI) changes that accompany aging. In general, appetite diminishes, the esophagus becomes less pliable (making food more difficult to swallow), gastritis and GI reflux disease (GIRD) make eating less pleasant, and problems with dentition may make chewing painful. Renal function also declines with age. The reduced ability of the kidneys to filter toxins from the body has numerous dietary implications.

As a result of aged-related physiological changes, many seniors have trouble maintaining their weight, so malnutrition, especially protein and total calorie deficiencies, become problematic. Being underweight and suffering rapid weight loss are independent predictors of mortality, particularly when weight loss is accompanied by functional impairments or complex psychological, social, and economic complications. These are the processes and issues that give us the "frail elderly."

Malnutrition can also contribute to impaired cognitive function (just as impaired cognitive function can give rise to malnutrition). Several vitamin deficiencies, particularly deficiencies of vitamins B12 and B6, and folate, are associated with cognitive impairment. Tracing causality in the other direction, impaired cognitive ability may interfere with the senior's ability to shop for or prepare food. "The decreased ability to prepare a meal, which may adversely affect an elderly patient's ability to ensure sufficient nourishment, has been cited as one of the earliest signs of mild cognitive impairment" (Wells and Dumbrell 2006:70). With advanced dementia comes forgetting to eat, even forgetting how to eat, and other nutritional compromises.

Since it is often difficult to separate clinical malnutrition from age-related changes in muscle mass, weight, and stature, estimates of the rate of malnutrition among the elderly are all over the map. About one in three seniors suffers from protein deficits, caloric insufficiency, one or more vitamin and mineral deficiencies, or some combination of these. Among institutionalized seniors, the figure might be as high as 50 or 60 percent. It is apparently not known how these figures vary depending on the level of food insecurity, but the reasonable assumption is that the less food-secure a person is, the more common these problems would be. There is certainly ample evidence to show that among food-insecure seniors, the intake of vital nutrients is reduced (Lee and Frongillo 2001; Ziliak, Gunderson, and Haist 2008); self-reported health status as well as observed physical and mental health decline (Lee and Frongillo 2001; Stuff et al. 2004; Ziliak, Gunderson, and Haist 2008); depression increases (Klesges et al. 2001; Kim and Frongillo 2007); and activities of daily living are restricted (Ziliak, Gunderson, and Haist 2008).

Nutritional Inadequacy

Research from the National Health and Nutrition Examination Surveys has shown that seniors experiencing food insecurity have a lower intake of major nutrients including but not limited to protein, vitamins A and C, iron, and calcium. Other research shows that food-insecure seniors are at an increased risk of diabetes, while seniors facing persistent (chronic, severe) food insecurity have a higher chance of being underweight and malnourished, even controlling for poverty, disease, functional impairments, education, age, gender, and race/ethnicity (Lee and Frongillo 2001; Ziliak, Gunderson, and Haist 2008). Analyses of senior hunger using the 1999–2003 Panel Study of Income Dynamics (PSID) further corroborate these results in that food-insecure seniors are less likely to report being in good health, have higher BMI scores, have higher rates of diabetes, and are more likely to be hospitalized than those who are food-secure (Ziliak, Gunderson, and Haist 2008).

Senior Food Shopping and Meal Preparation

Focus groups done by our research team with low-income seniors (many of them on the local Meals on Wheels waiting list) confirm that access to food is less of a barrier for most than the sheer hassle of shopping and preparing meals, a point recognized by all programs providing home-delivered meals. Most of our focus-group participants were senior women living alone, so their special challenge was cooking for a single person. Supermarket portion sizes are not optimal for a single person, or are much more expensive per unit when available. Cookware is not designed to cook for one either. Then there are the questions of leftovers, cleaning up, and so on. For many seniors, a bag of microwave popcorn and a can of soda suffice.

Most food-insecure seniors in Orange County (and in Florida in general) have microwave ovens, working cooktops and ranges, and at least some freezer capacity, so basic equipment for home meal preparation is not the problem. (These questions have not been asked in other surveys but we can assume they generalize.) But, to cite just one example, 27 percent of food-insecure Orange County seniors say that they have some difficulty preparing meals, and only one in four lives with someone who could help. About one in ten senior households in the county also contains at least one person younger than eighteen (presumably grandchildren). In short, a great deal of food insecurity among seniors has less to do with the availability of food than with difficulties shopping for, transporting, and preparing food for consumption. Economics are only part of the issue.

Participation of Seniors in Food Assistance Programs

According to the Food Research and Action Center (FRAC), older Americans who are eligible for SNAP are substantially *less* likely to participate than other groups because they are mistaken or uninformed about how much they will receive in benefits, are unaware of their eligibility, or recoil from the stigma associated with participation. Unless these challenges are overcome, the most helpful way to combat food insecurity among seniors may be through the nonprofit sector or through changes in state policies regarding benefit levels and eligibility requirements (Food Research and Action Center 2010). However, many food-insecure seniors are unaware of emergency food pantries in their own neighborhoods.

Some research shows that SNAP participation has positive effects on food security among the elderly, some shows negative effects, and some shows no effects at all. Even studies showing positive effects do not show *large* positive effects. Thus, whether there is much or little to be gained by increasing SNAP participation among income-eligible seniors is undetermined. Offsetting any positive gains are the documented confusion among seniors about eligibility requirements, the forms and paperwork (or computer sophistication) required for registering and re-registering, and if the benefits make the effort worthwhile. As one additional resource, SNAP probably has marginally positive effects for most, but even then the low benefit levels imply that participating seniors will still experience episodes when they do not have sufficient food. In other words, SNAP might increase the resources available for food without decreasing food insecurity.

Conclusion

Food insecurity, like war, "is not healthy for children and other living things." Studies of numerous populations using a variety of methodologies consistently show that food-insecure people have numerous physical and mental health deficits, even with all the obvious confounds held constant. The implications of these findings were spelled out by Senator Bernie Sanders, chairman of the Senate Subcommittee on Primary Health and Aging, in a report issued in 2011 titled *Senior Hunger: The Human Toll and Consequences.* Sanders's point was that if food insecurity leads to increased morbidity, as it clearly does, then it also leads to otherwise avoidable hospitalizations and probably some amount of premature mortality as well. What, then, are the economics of feeding people versus hospitalizing them? Sanders reports that the cost of one year of home-delivered meals is about equal to the cost of one day in the hospital. Food, in short, is cheap relative to health care.

4

Are Food Deserts the Source of the Problem?

The term "food desert" was first used in Scotland in the early 1990s (Cummins and Macintyre 1999) to refer to areas (neighborhoods, census tracts, communities, etc.) that lacked access to healthy, nutritious, and affordable food. Once conceptualized, it became obvious that food deserts were not distributed randomly across the landscape. Rather, they tended to be concentrated in low-income or minority neighborhoods. Could food deserts therefore be the cause of disparate dietary patterns and levels of food insecurity and health outcomes across races, economic classes, and geographic regions? Many people are convinced the answer is yes. We are not.

For such a seemingly simple question, no one has yet come up with a completely satisfactory answer. The very definition of a food desert has been debated; some have even wondered if such things exist. Do people who live in these "deserts" in fact eat a different diet or pay higher prices than people who live in areas where fresh, wholesome food is abundant? And if so, are the food deserts responsible for this or are other causal factors present? Would putting full-service supermarkets in the food deserts make a discernible difference in diets, health outcomes, or the overall rate of food insecurity?

According to the USDA, food deserts are "urban neighborhoods and rural towns without ready access to fresh, healthy, and affordable food. Instead of supermarkets and grocery stores, these communities may have no food access or are served only by fast food restaurants and convenience stores that offer few healthy, affordable food options" (US Department of Agriculture 2013). Using census tracts as the unit of aggregation, there are two further operational thresholds in the USDA definition: the tracts must be both low-income and low-access communities. Low-income means a poverty rate of 20 percent or greater or a median family income at or below 80 percent of the area median family income. Low access means that the tract contains at least 500 persons (or a third of the census tract's population) living more than one mile from a supermarket or large grocery store (ten miles in the case of nonmetropolitan census tracts).

This definition, now used more or less universally in food desert research, has been controversial since it was formulated (see, e.g., Wrigley, Warm, and Margetts 2002; Berg and Murdoch 2008; US Department of Agriculture 2009; Sparks, Bania, and Leete 2011; Franco 2015). First, food deserts are defined as census tracts, but tracts correspond only loosely with neighborhoods. Less than one US household in five purchases food in the same census tract where they live (Drewnowski, Aggarwal, and Vemez Moudon 2010; *The Economist* 2011; Aggarwal et al. 2014). Further, the standards used to define low-income tracts are arbitrary and hard to justify. The distance standards seem equally meaningless and are effectively trivial for households with cars. Is one mile assumed to be a reasonable walking distance? For seniors, children, the obese, the disabled, or anyone lugging a full bag of groceries, a one-mile walk would be a challenge. Finally, the nominal definition of a food desert specifies that these are areas "without ready access to fresh, healthy, and affordable food," but there is nothing in the operational definition that addresses fresh, healthy, or affordable. The apparent assumption is that there are no healthy options available in fast food restaurants and convenience stores, whereas fresh, healthy, and affordable foods abound in full-service supermarkets. But even McDonald's features numerous grilled chicken sandwiches, a couple of salads, fresh apple slices, and bottled water; many convenience stores and even gas stations stock items such as eggs, milk, some fresh fruit, cereal, trail mix, cheese, peanut butter, whole grain crackers, yogurt, and even hummus. As for the dizzying array of junk food, alcohol, soda pop, and other nutritional catastrophes that adorn every full-service supermarket in the United States, nothing further need be said.

The concern with food deserts in low-income communities is that residents of these areas experience a special type of food insecurity—

not that food is unavailable, but that the food is not nutritionally ade-quate and is overpriced. The unavailability of nutritious food is in turn linked to many health issues among residents of these areas (Andrews, Bhatta, and Ver Ploeg 2013). Whether these health issues are a direct result of living in food deserts or a result of the characteristics of peo-ple who happen to live in such areas (poor, racial minorities, etc.) is a key question we take up later.

Theories of Food Desert Formation

Researchers have proposed different theories to explain how food deserts emerged in the United States. One of the most popular is that chain supermarket stores have put smaller, neighborhood "mom and pop" grocery stores out of business (Guy, Clarke, and Eyre 2004). But these suburban mega-supermarkets are only available to those with cars or those who can get to them via public transportation. Without transportation, many are left to do their grocery shopping at convenience stores where nutritious food is less available and more expensive (Hendrickson, Smith, and Eikenberry 2006). Food insecurity among the urban poor is the result.

Other researchers have argued that food deserts arose in inner-city areas because the median income dropped when affluent residents migrated to suburban areas in the 1960s through the 1980s (Wienk 1979; Bianchi, Farley, and Spain 1982; Nyden et al. 1998; Flournoy 2006; Walker, Keane, and Burke 2010). Migration to the suburbs caused half the supermarkets in the three largest cities of the United States to close (Diesenhouse 1993; Miller 1994; Alwitt and Donley 1997; Walker, Keane, and Burke 2010). The same migration caused a significant decrease in the median income of the inner-city areas, which equates to less purchasing power and fewer stores. Amanda Shaffer (2002) explored this process and found that middle- and upper-income (and white) suburban communities (in California) had twice as many supermarkets as low-income (and black) communities.

Other studies analyzing access to grocery stores in communities by racial composition and poverty have produced similar findings (e.g., Powell et al. 2007a). Kimberly Morland, Steve Wing, and Ana Roux (2002) collected data on the dietary intake of residents partici-pating in the Atherosclerosis Risk in Communities study to examine the local food environment's impact on nutrition. These communities were located in Maryland, North Carolina, Mississippi, and Minnesota. Predominantly white census tracts had five times the number of supermarkets that black neighborhoods had. Findings were similar in a study by Shannon Zenk and colleagues (2005) examining the accessibility to food stores by income level and racial composition of neighborhoods in Detroit. Residents of high-income and white neighborhoods had greater access to supermarkets and large chain food stores. Low-income and nonwhite neighborhoods had mostly small grocery and convenience stores.

Compared to suburban areas, land prices in urban areas are high and often only small plots are available. This makes it more expensive to build large supermarkets in urban areas (Alwitt and Donley 1997; Walker, Keane, and Burke 2010). In order to profit, supermarkets must move large quantities of goods. This is difficult in urban communities where population density is high but poverty is also high. The optimal combination of land, affluence, and people is found in the suburbs, and that is where the supermarkets tend to be ("Grocery Store Development" 2012).

Despite some variation in the details, all theories depict food deserts as the creation of voracious, profit-maximizing capitalism and as responsible, at least partly, for food insecurity. The large supermarket chains and the many ancillary businesses that sustain them (distribution, marketing, production, etc.) see themselves less in the business of feeding the world and more in the business of generating profit. The money is in the suburbs (mainly) and so that is where the stores want to be. As political commentator Matt Bruenig (2012) put it, "Why do food deserts exist? [Because] poor people do not have very much money."

One food activist in the South Bronx (Fields 2013) objects to the current conceptualization of food deserts as places that lack convenient access to full-service supermarkets because this idea "proposes large corporate grocery stores as the solution and often doesn't encapsulate the reasons why these black-and-white solutions are so difficult" in low-income communities. The real problem, here and everywhere, "is poverty, and solutions should be community-based rather than corporate." It does seem fair to ask why more full-service supermarkets are the answer to a problem that is largely the result of business decisions of the full-service supermarket chains. But if that is not the right answer, then what is?

Do Food Deserts Even Exist?

Many census tracts satisfy the USDA definition of a food desert—in fact, 6,529 of them do, about 9 percent of all tracts. Three-fourths of these tracts are urban, and an estimated 13.6 million food-insecure people live within them. But does the USDA definition of a food desert demarcate a real and serious problem? If a census tract lacks a large full-service supermarket, does that imply that there are no food outlets other than fast food restaurants and convenience stores that only offer shelves of unhealthy food? One alternative is small full-service grocery stores, such as the Adam's Oakland Market in East Oakland (one of three sites included in a 2007 study by Short, Guthman, and Raskin). "Food systems researchers and activists have paid scant attention to studying the potential role of small full-service retail food stores. . . . These stores meet many of the criteria for community food security . . . by providing a wide variety of relatively low-cost foods" (p. 352). Also overlooked are the tens of thousands of larger and smaller food retailers, farmers' markets, corner groceries, roadside food vendors, bodegas, and such, many of which specialize in fresh produce, locally grown meat, fish, and dairy, or in short, fresh, healthy food. Contrary to the widespread impression, these not-large food retailers and specialty shops collectively account for almost half the total US food market.

The Short, Guthman, and Raskin study was carried out in three low-income communities in San Francisco and Oakland. All qualified as food deserts because there was no large full-service supermarket in any of them. Two of the three communities had large supermarkets within half a mile of the neighborhood perimeter, and the third had one large discount market and a mid-sized market within its borders. All but one also had numerous mid-sized and small food markets dispersed throughout the neighborhood. Of the three (all identified by USDA criteria as food deserts), there was only one "where food availability seems to be a serious problem" (Short, Guthman, and Raskin 2007:357).

Surely these small and medium-sized markets are more expensive and carry low-quality or no fresh produce, little better than the convenience stores. Are they not high-cost nutritional wastelands? The data say otherwise. First, "the prices at all three of the small markets in the Mission and the medium sized grocery store in Bayview had substantially lower prices than the nearby chain stores. Across all stores studied and all food items examined, prices in general were either lower or about the same as prices at nearby national chains. As for quality, the study examined fresh produce available in the markets and compared the results to those at nearby national chains. In one case, produce quality was clearly lower (more wilted veggies, more over-ripe and bruised fruits, etc.), but in all other cases the produce quality was rated by observers as excellent or at least 'good,' comparable to the quality ratings in the chains. It was also clear that "small stores can and do offer foods necessary for nutritionally adequate diets, as described by the Thrifty Food Plan" (Short, Guthman, and Raskin 2007:359) and that the small neighborhood food markets easily outdo the big chains in offering more culturally appropriate foods.

What we learn from the San Francisco Bay Area study is that in at least some cases, the food situation in certain neighborhoods is probably not as dire as the designation "food desert" suggests. Another study, undertaken in Boston, underscores that point (Walker, Block, and Kawachi 2012). These authors used concept mapping to ascertain local perceptions of food price and availability in neighborhoods identified as food deserts, and compared those perceptions to the equivalent perceptions in "food oases" (where high-quality food is abundant). This led to a measure of food-buying practices, which turned out to be largely the same in both food deserts and food oases. People whose food-buying practices led them to the junk food aisles tended to buy junk food even if they were around the corner from a large supermarket; and people whose food-buying practices led them to seek out fresh produce and dairy also did so even if it entailed a long ride on the bus. Food-buying practices were similar between residents of food deserts and residents of food oases.

Likewise, a study from the United Kingdom (Pearson et al. 2005) calculated distances to the nearest supermarket for a sample of a thousand postal addresses to which questionnaires were sent. The questionnaires asked about grocery prices, prior-day consumption of fruits and vegetables, potential difficulties with shopping, and other factors. Produce prices, distance to the nearest supermarket, and potential difficulties shopping for groceries were not significantly associated with either fruit or vegetable consumption. In this study, the three most common descriptors of a food desert—high cost of fruits and vegetables, socioeconomic deprivation, and lack of local supermarkets—were not significant factors predicting fruit or vegetable intake.

One of the better studies of the relationship between "neighbor-hood food environment" and dietary intake is that by An Ruopeng and Roland Sturm (2012). These analysts looked at self-reported diets of some 13,500 California children and adolescents. Dietary measures were based on "daily servings of fruits, vegetables, juice, milk, soda, high-sugar foods, and fast food, which were regressed on measures of food environments. Food environments were measured by counts and density of businesses, distinguishing fast-food restaurants, convenience stores, small food stores, grocery stores, and large supermarkets within a specific distance" (p. 129). Making a long story short, no major relationship between food environment and consumption was found. The results did not support the hypothesis that more supermarkets or fewer fast food outlets and convenience stores within walking distance would improve diets or lower BMIs. Victoria Shier, An Ruopeng, and Roland Sturm (2012) concluded, based on the Early Childhood Longitudinal Study–Kindergarten Cohort (ECLS-K) survey data for more than 6,000 US eighth-graders all over the United States, that increased access to large supermarkets did not result in lower youth BMI. They also found that a greater concentration of fast food restaurants, convenience stores, and small food stores did not correlate to an increase in BMI, as many other studies have also found.

But so too are there many studies that reach opposite conclusions, studies whose results indicate that residents of food deserts do eat poorer diets. Brennan Davis and Christopher Carpenter (2009) studied California children but used data from the California Healthy Kids survey and found a positive relationship between nearness of fast food restaurants to a child's school and both soda consumption and obesity. Likewise, Deja Hendrickson, Chery Smith, and Nicole Eikenberry (2006) studied residents in four low-income communities, two urban and two rural, in Minnesota. The results of their food inventory showed that the foods that were available in the communities were expensive, of fair or poor quality, and that they were limited in both number and variety. This was correlated with an inability for residents to access foods that would help them maintain a healthy lifestyle.

A study (Gallagher 2006) based on Chicago's 18,888 census blocks or block groups calculated the distance from every Chicago block to the nearest grocery store and fast food restaurant and on that basis identified Chicago's food deserts. As always, the blocks so designated were disproportionally nonwhite and low-income; in fact, Chicago's food deserts are nearly exclusively in black communities. The findings "point to one conclusion: communities that have no or distant grocery stores, or have an imbalance of healthy food options, will likely have increased premature death and chronic health conditions, holding other influences constant. . . . [I]t is clear that food deserts, especially those with an abundance of fast food options, pose serious health and wellness challenges to the residents who live within them and to the City of Chicago as a whole" (p. 9).

Researchers frequently encounter literatures where one study concludes X and another concludes not-X, and so to the question "Which is it?" the only honest answer is, "It depends!"—not a satisfactory answer but the only honest answer available. Some general points of criticism pertinent to most or all studies follow.

First, food deserts are always populated by relatively poor, nonwhite populations, and they are distinctive in many other ways as well (percent of abandoned housing, local crime rate, low education, high unemployment, etc.). Absent statistical controls for these demographic and socioeconomic factors, not much of value can be concluded, as we generally cannot decide which outcomes are the result of living in a particular place (the "neighborhood food environment") and which are the result of social, demographic, and economic variables that happen to be correlated with living in particular places. The observed relationships, that is, may be spurious, not "real." Single-site case studies are particularly deficient in this regard.

Second, even if it can be shown that a particular relationship is real, correlation is not cause. If people who live in food deserts eat too much junk food and not enough fresh produce, that does not necessarily mean that their unhealthy diets are the result of living in a food desert. For all we know, their diets might be equally deficient even if they lived across the street from a full-service supermarket.

And third, the studies rarely specify why one set of research sites was chosen rather than another, and this raises the specter of observer bias—that is, the possibility that sites are chosen, whether consciously or not, to sustain a theoretical conclusion, not based on empirical observation, to which the investigator is already committed. With a little digging, anyone can locate a neighborhood or two in any US city that completely fulfills the food desert stereotype—poor, black neighborhoods whose streets are lined with gas stations, convenience stores, fried chicken restaurants, fast food franchises, drug dealers, hookers, and disaffected teens. And with near certainty, one will also find high rates of obesity, diabetes, premature mortality, and severe food insecurity in these same places. But with equal ease, one can also find other low-income neighborhoods, equally poor, equally black, and equally distraught, that also have an organic fruit and vegetable stand, a health food store, or a large grocery store that people from other communities drive miles to shop at (*The Economist* 2011). One can, in short, find anecdotal evidence—cases of uncertain generalizability—to support nearly anything.

Race and Class Disparities in Access to Healthy Food

We know that food insecurity is highest in low-income families and among racial and ethnic minorities, the same populations that are overrepresented in USDA-defined food deserts. Thus, there is no disputing that there are racial, ethnic, and class disparities in access to adequate food. The issue is not whether this is true but why. Is it exclusively a matter of retail locations (place)? Is it mainly a matter of economics? In what ways does "culture" fit into the mix?

It is well known that there are correlations between living in food deserts, eating poor diets, and suffering from chronic diseases. The issue is whether these correlations bespeak cause. The assumption throughout the literature on food deserts is that if the people living in food deserts were somehow given access to better food, they would buy it and be healthier as a result. But what if this assumption is wrong? While there are some exceptions, most studies suggest that the assumption is indeed wrong. Specifically, the diets of dwellers of food deserts do not tend to improve very much, or at all, when better food and different food outlets are made available. This literature intimates that the dietary issues and food insecurities that beset poor, black communities are generally not the result of neighborhood food-retailer locations.

The most recent study to reach this conclusion is by Brian Elbel and colleagues (2015), undertaken in Brooklyn by a research team from New York University. Under the auspices of the New York City's Food Retail Expansion to Support Health (FRESH) and with funding from the federal Healthy Food Financing Initiative, a community in the South Bronx (Morrisania), a largely black and Hispanic community with high poverty rates and one of the worst health profiles of any community in the city, was chosen as the site for a new, large (17,000-square-foot), full-service supermarket. A demographically similar nearby community, Highbridge, was selected as the comparison community. Detailed data on dietary intakes were collected from parents and caregivers of children ages three to ten in the several months leading up to the new store's opening in August 2011, then again in the two months following the opening, and then approximately one year later.

The design is a "natural experiment." If the absence of a full-service supermarket in a neighborhood causes people to eat suboptimal diets, then opening one should cause dietary behaviors to improve. So the prediction would be significant changes in diet, consumption, and purchasing behavior subsequent to the store's opening, if not immediately then surely within a year. Also, since advocacy groups have been urging people to eat better diets for years, a comparison community ensures that any changes observed in the "treatment" condition are not common trends occurring everywhere. As nonrandomized or quasi-experimental designs go, this one is fairly sound.

The findings were unequivocal. "While there were small, inconsistent changes over the time periods, there were no appreciable differences in availability of healthful or unhealthful foods at home, or in children's dietary intake as a result of the supermarket. . . . The introduction of a government-subsidized supermarket into an underserved neighborhood in the Bronx did not result in significant changes in household food availability or children's dietary intake" (Elbel et al. 2015:2881). One commentator on the study (Taylor 2015) remarked, "Increasing access to fresh food does not guarantee that people have the money, let alone the time and knowledge, to take advantage of it."

A similar study (Cummins, Flint, and Matthews 2014) looked for the effects of opening a new full-service supermarket in a food desert community in Philadelphia. The authors found that there were moderate gains in terms of accessibility to food, but no changes were reported in fruit and vegetable intake or in BMI. Based on these findings, the authors questioned the widely held belief that increasing access to healthy food by locating a grocery store in a community leads to positive changes in diet and BMI.

Another study (Hattori, An, and Sturm 2013) analyzed data on almost 100,000 adults who completed the 2007 and 2009 California Health Interview Surveys. The ultimate outcome variables were all derived from BMI measures. Other variables were the number of times per week that fruits, vegetables, sugar-sweetened soft drinks, fried potatoes, and fast food were consumed; the number of fast food restaurants, full-service restaurants, convenience stores, small food stores, grocery stores, and large supermarkets that were within varying distances (0.25 to 3.0 miles) from the survey respondent's residence; and the usual socio-demographic controls. The findings were mixed. Being located close to fast food restaurants was correlated with an increase in eating fast food and drinking sodas as well as the probability of being overweight or obese. However, proximity to fast food outlets was not correlated with BMI.

Similar results were obtained by Janne Boone-Heinonen and colleagues (2011) based on fifteen years of data from the Coronary Artery Risk Development in Young Adults (CARDIA) study. As with the 2013 Hattori, An, and Sturm study, the Boone-Heinonen study showed that eating fast food was clearly associated with fast food availability among low-income respondents (men much more than women). However, diet quality and the intake of fruits and vegetables were not generally correlated with an increase in supermarket access.

To determine if there is a link between local food availability and obesity among young children, Helen Lee (2012) analyzed data from the Early Childhood Longitudinal Study–Kindergarten Cohort. "I find that children who live in residentially poor and minority neighborhoods are indeed more likely to have greater access to fast-food outlets and convenience stores. However, these neighborhoods also have greater access to other food establishments that have not been linked to increased obesity risk, including large-scale grocery stores. When examined in a multi-level modeling framework, differential exposure to food outlets does not independently explain weight gain over time in this sample of elementary school-aged children. Variation in residential food outlet availability also does not explain socioeconomic and racial/ethnic differences. It may thus be important to reconsider whether food access is, in all settings, a salient factor in understanding obesity risk among young children" (p. 1193).

These findings were anticipated in a review essay published in *Obesity Reviews* (White 2007) on the topic of food accessibility and obesity. Although Martin White focused on United Kingdom studies, plenty of US studies were also reviewed. One section of the paper dealt with food deserts, at the time a rather new concept. "The idea of food deserts had immediate appeal to the media and policymakers, and rapidly became enshrined in government policy; it was mentioned in the [United Kingdom] National Health Strategy and the Government's independent enquiry into health inequalities. However, it is important to recognize that it has *little scientific basis*" (p. 100, emphasis added). Studies of food availability are a morass of contradictions. Some show higher quality and lower prices in the large supermarkets, but "more recent studies have failed to replicate these findings, showing instead that 'healthy' foods tend to be as, if not more, available in poorer areas and are lower in price" (p. 101). With respect to distance versus mode of transit: "This research consistently demonstrates that car ownership and use of a car to buy food is socioeconomically patterned and that this is a key determinant in choice of main food stores" (p. 101).

Does retail access affect what we eat? Three types of research designs have been used to address this question: ecological studies (looking for correlations between some measure of food access in a geographical area and some measure of diet, obesity, or health indicators in the same geographic areas); individual-level studies (studies based on cross-sectional surveys that correlate food access and diet at the individual versus ecological levels); and experimental studies (such as the quasi-experiment in Brooklyn described earlier). The more persuasive and better-designed studies tend to show that food retail access alone does not have a significant effect on a person's diet (Dubowitz et al. 2014; White 2007).

In conclusion, a causal link between access to full-service supermarkets and dietary health has yet to be established. As one commentator put it in *The Economist* (2011): "Merely improving access to healthy food does not change consumer behavior. Open a full-service supermarket in a food desert and shoppers tend to buy the same artery-clogging junk food as before—they just pay less for it. The unpalatable truth seems to be that some Americans simply do not care to eat a balanced diet, while others, increasingly, cannot afford to."

Not owning a car is a much more serious barrier than the distance to the nearest supermarket. All studies confirm that very few people (on the order of 10–15 percent) shop for groceries in the same census tract (or neighborhood) where they live, so the very definition of a "food desert" is questionable. Cultural background, tradition, education, custom, and habit are far more telling predictors of what people choose to eat than how far they are from the nearest full-service supermarket or how many fast food outlets and convenience stores they pass along the way.

The food desert literature often assumes that food deserts matter because consumers "make decisions on their food intake based on the food available to them in their neighborhood. In food deserts, it is typical for residents to purchase their food at the local convenience store" (Donley and Gualtieri 2015:287). But the persistence of unhealthy food choices in the food deserts seems to reflect factors other than just retail food locations. Three hypotheses suggest themselves. First, many people are uneducated about nutrition and make poor food choices even when they don't have to. Second, people know what the healthy options are but can't afford to buy healthy food. And third, food choices are more a function of custom, habit, tradition, and culture than they are the result of nutrition information, economic constraints, or market locations. In all likelihood, all of these play a role.

Convenience Stores

A subtext throughout the literature on food deserts is that the food available in convenience stores is a nutritional disaster. A recent story in the *Greenville News* (South Carolina) (Callum-Penso 2014) suggests that this may be changing. The story is based on an interview with Jeff Lenard, a vice president for strategic industry initiatives with the National Association of Convenience Stores. As Lenard is an industry spokesperson, one must treat his assessments with caution, but his interview intimates that today's convenience stores feature more healthful options than in decades past. "Back then [the specific reference is 1983], convenience stores were seen as places of desperation—not destination—for food. And today they are destination," a place where people can go for fresh fruit and veggies, dairy products, and other unlikely food products.

Driving the movement toward more fresh and wholesome food is not a newfound sense of social responsibility but economics. For decades, the two biggest sellers in the convenience store portfolio were tobacco and gasoline. Sales of both have declined markedly and fresh food has become a replacement product. "Somewhere along the line, gas stations began to get the message—people want food." And not just the prepackaged, high fat, salty, and sugary snack items that convenience stores have always sold, but rather fresh, nutritious, healthy food. More and more, the convenience stores have come to resemble markets that happen to sell gas, not gas stations where you can buy a few food items. The nutritional advantages of full-service supermarkets over convenience stores, it seems, may be diminishing.

(That said, it is still a simple matter to find convenience stores particularly in low-income areas that amply fulfill every stereotype of the nutritional wasteland.)

Why Are the Poor Relatively Undernourished?

We just enunciated three testable hypotheses for why poor people have poor diets and equally poor health outcomes such as obesity, diabetes, and heart disease, none of which have anything to do with food deserts: they don't know any better; they can't afford to eat healthy food; and culture, custom, and tradition dictate what people eat, but the food culture, customs, and traditions of the poor tend to favor unhealthy food. There are substantial although not conclusive research literatures on all three points.

Class, Race, and Nutritional Knowledge

Unless you possess rudimentary nutritional information, it is not immediately obvious that an apple is a better snack choice than a bag of potato chips or a Snickers bar. The educational deficits of schools serving poor and minority populations are well known. Nutritional knowledge among low-income and minority populations might therefore be lacking, at least in comparison to affluent whites.

Several studies can be found to support this conclusion. Patricia Cluss and colleagues (2013) studied nutritional knowledge among parents of Medicaid-insured obese children and concluded that being black, having less education, and being very low-income were associated with poorer nutrition knowledge. Parents of these children tended to believe that foods were healthier than they in fact were. Another study (Slusser et al. 2012) surveyed a sample of urban low-income, low-education Latino immigrants with preschool-age children and reported a significant relationship between low nutrition knowledge and less healthy child-feeding practices.

Other studies though lead to different conclusions. Both Elizabeth Lynch and colleagues (2012) and Sean Lucan and colleagues (2012) studied concepts of healthy foods and healthy diets among low-income African Americans. Lynch and colleagues found that low-income African American women generally had accurate understandings of which foods were healthful and which were not but lacked awareness of why some foods were healthier than others. Lucan and colleagues undertook largely unstructured interviews with low-income blacks in a community in west Philadelphia, whose "participants generally expressed views consistent with nutritional guidelines and dietary recommendations that were in place at the time of our study. Participants discussed dietary concepts in ways, and using terminology, that most nutrition authorities would not challenge" (p. 758).

Irene Acheampong and Lauren Haldeman (2013) studied nutrition attitudes, knowledge, and beliefs among low-income black and Hispanic women and found that the majority of black participants possessed good knowledge of nutrition while Hispanics had fair knowledge. They also found that among both groups, the most common barrier to eating a healthy diet was the cost of healthy foods, not the knowledge of what constitutes a healthy diet. Another study of note is Laura-Anne Minkoff-Zern's analysis of California farmworkers. She notes that "food assistance providers in the USA often treat farmworkers' inability to afford healthy food as a lack of knowledge about healthy eating, reinforcing racialized assumptions that people of color don't know 'good' food" (2012). The assumption, in short, is that racial and ethnic minorities and the poor make "bad" food choices because they don't know any better. Minkoff-Zern's analysis shows instead that "food security and healthy eating, rather than being a matter of consumers making healthy 'choices,' is a matter of class-based and racial differences in the food system" (p. 1190). Rather than assuming that proper education about nutrition would solve the food problems of the poor, her insistence is that income inequality is the heart of the matter, a point we argue throughout this volume.

The Economics of Eating Healthy

As people who shop at farmers' markets or health food stores such as Fresh Market or Whole Foods will agree, healthy eating is indeed more expensive. High-quality protein is more expensive than canned pasta products, fresh fruits and veggies are more expensive than frozen produce, and so on (Krisberg 2013). But what does contemporary food science say about the difference?

The best recent study of the topic is by Mayuree Rao and colleagues (2013), a meta-analysis of twenty-seven prior studies chosen because each reported average prices for foods that were characterized according to healthfulness. On average, healthier diets cost about $1.48 more per person per day.

A dollar and a half may not seem like a lot of money, but within the food budget of the poor it is not trivial. In 2013, the poverty line for a family of four was $23,050. Adding $1.50 per day for 365 days times four people amounts to $2,190 per year. So going from a less healthy to more healthy diet would add 9.5 percent to the annual cost of living for a four-person family right at the poverty line, and even higher percentage increases for families below the poverty line. A family of four whose annual income was half the poverty line (annual income of $11,525) would see their annual cost of living increase by 19 percent by switching from a less healthy to more healthy diet. Or consider the increased cost of a healthy diet from the viewpoint of SNAP. An adult male is considered SNAP-eligible if his weekly food budget (one-third of income) is $35 per week or less. Adding $1.50 a day for seven days in a week amounts to $10.50— an increase in weekly cost of living of about a third.

A related study in the United Kingdom (Jones et al. 2014) used longitudinal data to examine food prices over time. The trend indicator was the cost per 1,000 kilocalories. In 2012, the average price per 1,000 kilocalories was *three times higher* for the healthiest diet than for the least-healthful diet. Further analysis confirmed that from 2002 to 2012, all food prices had risen but the price of healthy food had risen faster.

Pablo Monsivais and Adam Drewnowski (2007) compared prices for 372 foods and changes in the prices over a two-year period. Foods were categorized from lower energy density to higher energy density. Low-energy-density foods include whole grains, lean meats, low-fat dairy products, and vegetables and fruits; high-energy-density foods are mainly sweets and fats. The results showed, first, that low-energy-dense (healthier) foods were far more expensive per calorie provided than high-energy-dense foods (by an order of magnitude), and second, that the cost of healthier foods had increased far more rapidly than the cost of less healthy foods. Replacing fats and sweets with healthier options is increasingly becoming a more difficult economic challenge.

The economics of eating are pretty straightforward. The poor gravitate toward high-sugar, high-fat, and cheap but unhealthful diets. As Monsivais and Drewnowski conclude, "The finding that energy-dense foods are not only the least expensive, but also most resistant to inflation, may also help explain why the highest rates of obesity continue to be observed among groups of limited economic means" (2007:2071). This does not imply that the poor are predestined to eat unhealthy diets. Aggressively cautious food purchasing and preparation could lead to better diets even if incomes did not increase. But doing so increases the time and effort required to shop for and prepare food, and for many poor people, other factors such as satiation, limited time, convenience, and familiarity are of greater importance.

Class, Race, and Food Cultures

Factors in food choices other than health and price (assumed to be universal motivators) result either from previous personal experiences or from differences in culture, custom, habit, and food traditions. Culture is a huge factor in determining what we think is appropriate to eat. Culture can determine what parts of an animal may or may not be eaten, how and when food is prepared, and what is considered healthful or tasty. Rebecca Hubbard and colleagues (2014) analyzed how culture can impact food choices. They found that participants identifying as Asian, African American, or Hispanic scored significantly higher on their measures of connection (the presumed importance of food in one's culture) and social value (how important food is believed to be in one's culture) than white individuals did. Additionally, African American and white participants were more likely to rate their cultural foods as healthy than Asian and Hispanic participants. Thus among some groups, while culturally important foods may not be viewed as healthy, they may still be viewed as important parts of cultural identity.

A point often overlooked by today's "eat healthy" advocates is that from the beginning of time until maybe forty years ago, the leading nutritional problem was getting adequate calories *into* the human diet, not getting them out. Food cultures and traditions evolved around this central issue but now come into conflict with modern-day sedentary lifestyles. The cultural problem here, while malleable, will not just go away. Many elements of traditional cooking and food culture are nutritionally suboptimal but persist because food carries cultural identity and people cling to these identities even when healthier alternatives exist. Meat consumption, to cite an obvious example, has always been a marker of status. Many people struggle with the advice to eat more veggies and less meat, regardless of the wisdom of this advice.

Conclusion

Evidence from a variety of sources confirms that culture and economics are far greater barriers to healthy eating than the distance to the nearest full-service supermarket. This conclusion is now sustained by a sufficiently large number of studies that make one wonder whether "neighborhood food retail location" matters very much at all.

One serious issue with the "food desert" concept is that it does not lead to any plausible solution. The theory of the food desert is that people living in neighborhoods without access to a full-service supermarket will be more food-insecure and eat a worse diet than others, so the obvious solution would be to encourage more full-service supermarkets to open in food deserts. But the main reason they are not already there is because it is difficult to make a profit providing food to low-income populations. Efforts to overcome the economics have not been encouraging. Even when supermarkets (or other presumably healthier food outlets) do open in previously underserved areas, local food choices and food buying habits generally do not change.

Many other alternatives to locating full-service supermarkets in poor areas have been suggested, but none seem promising. Some suggest community gardens, community-supported agriculture, farmers' markets, and urban agriculture, but studies reviewed in the next chapter suggest that these interventions would not be very effective in turning food deserts into food oases.

Overcoming cultural resistance to dietary change is presumably a matter of better education, and surely the dietary knowledge of the average American could be improved. But there is not a lot of evidence suggesting that poor diets result from inadequate knowledge, and a small mountain of evidence that economics lies at the heart of the matter. For most, a lousy diet results from inadequate income far more often than from deficient knowledge or distance to a full-service grocery store. As Matt Bruenig (2012) puts it, "The food justice advocates have the entire thing backwards. The same thing that causes food deserts to exist is what causes them to persist—in effect—even when supermarkets come into the area. It is not proximity to grocery stores that matters; it is income. Providing the poor with higher incomes will eliminate food deserts and increase their genuine access—not just geographical access—to healthy foods."

5

Can People Solve
Their Own Food Insecurities?

Amartya Sen's (1981) analysis of food, economics, and enti-tlements reminds us that people can entitle themselves to food in two ways: the conversion of wealth or income into food, or direct production of food. Much of our book has focused on the former, but here we shift attention to the latter. If people need more food, why don't they just grow it? Is that not at least a partial solution?

Home and community gardening figure prominently in the discourse of the alternative-food movement (Grauerholz and Owens 2015), although not often as a solution to food insecurity. Rather, home and community gardening are promoted as an antidote to industrial agriculture (or "factory farming"). The reaction of the alternative-food movement to industrial agriculture embraces an entire ethic of food, an ideology surrounding the production, distribution, and consumption of food that ultimately interrogates global sustainability, animal rights, physical and mental well-being, the conservation of biodiversity, climate change, and protection and restoration of the planet's natural environment. Our concern here is simply whether home and community gardening could make a significant dent in the food-insecurity problem.

From the beginning of agriculture 10,000 years ago until the 1950s, home gardens were commonplace in poor, working, and even middle-class neighborhoods around the world. At the end of World

War II, hardly anyone was more than one or two generations "off the farm," so knowledge about working the land and growing food was widespread. Planting the garden was a spring ritual. Weeding the garden, fertilizing, fighting insects, and tending to the plants were weekly chores. Then came the harvest and with it weeks of canning, pickling, and otherwise preserving the garden's bounty.

Full-service supermarkets already existed by the 1950s, of course, but they were often inconvenient and not cheap. The first true supermarket was opened in 1930 in Queens, New York. Widespread proliferation of this new style of food marketing awaited the growth of the suburbs and automobile ownership after World War II. In many prewar neighborhoods, the larger share of commercial food was purchased at nearby corner groceries. These little stores had one significant advantage that the supermarkets lacked: they were willing to advance credit, a significant advantage for families living a hand-to-mouth existence. By the mid-1960s, however, the colonization of America's cities and towns by the large supermarket chains was well under way. Soon, weekly trips to the supermarket became the food acquisition norm.

As the supermarkets proliferated, national affluence increased, and with affluence came a need to display newfound status—in the choice of cars, in where and how one shopped, and especially in the grandeur of the home and yard. Well-manicured lawns pushed out home gardens as the principal feature of the American backyard. Swing-sets replaced tomato plants, barbecue grills replaced the lettuce and radish patch, and supermarket produce and groceries replaced the homegrown, home-canned, home-preserved product. It would be four decades before the appeal of home gardening returned.

Even at the height of their popularity, home gardens would have contributed only a small share of the family's food supply, mainly vegetables and perhaps some fruit, but no dry goods—flour, sugar, rice, salt; no dairy products—butter, milk, cheese, cream; and no meat. Given the typical American diet then and now, backyard produce could only have been a supplemental food source.

How supplemental? No firm data seem to exist on this topic. John Taylor and Sarah Lovell (2015) report a recent case study of urban home gardens that illustrates the weaknesses of the gardening literature. The case is based on thirty-one African American, Chinese, and Mexican home gardeners in Chicago who were identified through the aerial image analysis capabilities of Google Earth. The hypothesis was that urban home food gardens would "make a substantial contribution to household food budgets and to community food systems," but this could not be definitively evaluated because of methodological issues. First, noncompliance with the study's measurement demands was high. Estimated productivity based on average yield was also compromised because of the heterogeneity of the soils, variation in growing conditions, and the amount of water and shade. Thus, garden productivity could be analyzed only anecdotally. Some participants stated that their garden made a significant positive impact on their household food budget. How significant is unstated.

A systematic review of the gardening literature by Daniela Guitart, Catherine Pickering, and Jason Byrne (2012) discusses both motivations to garden and the benefits of doing so. "To consume [more] fresh foods" was the most common motivation mentioned but was only third on the list of "commonly demonstrated benefits," after "social development or cohesion" and "enhanced health." The authors note that benefits were more often asserted than demonstrated. "For example, improving nutrition by increasing fruit and vegetable intake was a benefit that was often mentioned in the literature but in some instances could not be demonstrated because of the complexity of evidence required in this field of study. There were often differences between the benefits mentioned and those demonstrated" (p. 10).

A study by William Hlubik and colleagues (1994; see Armstrong 2000 for discussion) found that community gardeners reduced their food cost by only $50 to $250 per season. Converting the higher number to current dollars would give $387 as the upper limit of what a home garden would yield. The minimum wage in Florida as of 2016 was $8.05 per hour, so gardening to save $387 in food costs would be rational if gardening consumed forty-eight or fewer hours per season.

That $387 can be looked at another way. In 2014, the US federal poverty line for a family of four was $23,880. The calculation of the poverty line assumes that poor families spend a third of their income on food. A third of $23,880 is $7,960 and $387 amounts to 4.9 percent of that. So at the upper limit, a household right at the poverty line could realize maybe a 5 percent reduction in food costs by putting in a garden. Larger gardens and more efficient gardening strategies might increase this number to as much as a tenth but probably not much more.

Advocates of the alternative-food movement respond by pointing out that home gardens *could* supply a much larger percentage of the diet if people would foreswear meat, dairy, other animal products, and all processed food and eat a natural, organic, vegetarian, or vegan diet instead. That the world must shift toward a plant-based organic diet to avoid environmental catastrophe is a key tenet in the ideology of the alternative-food movement. But as Julie Guthman has noted, "In assuming the universal goodness of fresh, local and organic food, those who value this food ask those who appear to reject this food to either be subject to conversion efforts or simply be deemed as 'other'" (p. 271). The argument for plant-based diets ignores the food preferences of 95 percent of the US population.

Community Gardens

For a variety of reasons (zoning and building codes, local ordinances, homeowner associations, cultural preferences), backyard gardens are not nearly as common as they were in the 1950s, so some advocates of the alternative-food movement have turned instead to community gardens—typically larger plots of land worked by multiple families. Community gardens can be made up of multiple individual plots or one community plot at a school, park, nursing home, community center, or even a vacant lot. Indeed, people who garden in vacant and abandoned lots are known as "guerrilla gardeners," folk heroes in the alternative-food movement.

Many communities create these gardens specifically to increase access to affordable, fresh, and healthy produce (Litt et al. 2011). Low-income neighborhoods in both rural and urban areas sometimes have limited access to full-service grocery stores, and this can make fresh fruits and vegetables difficult to access and afford (Himmel-green et al. 2000; Frongillo and Horan 2004; Huang, Oshima, and Kim 2010). As a result, some communities start community gardens to give residents opportunities to grow their own produce and reduce food costs (Armstrong 2000; Baker 2004). How successful they are at this is a key question.

Besides growing food, many community gardens are intended to serve as educational tools. This aim articulates a key premise of the alternative-food movement, that if people only knew where their food comes from, they would demand more local and organic food and be willing to pay for it. The premise is that any honest description of industrial agriculture would have a very high "yuck" factor and would trigger an immediate desire for alternative food (see Guth-man 2008). Again, whether community gardening has this effect is an important question. Some gardens are also aimed at providing ther-apy, encouraging a healthier lifestyle, or building social capital.

Guitart, Pickering, and Byrne (2012) reviewed eighty-seven aca-demic papers on community gardens published between 1985 and 2011. Most of these papers discussed the motivations behind estab-lishing community gardens and they are generally in accord with what we have just stated. The most commonly cited motivations were to consume more fresh foods, to build community, to improve health outcomes among participants, to save money on produce, and to gen-erate money from selling produce from the garden. Secondary but still common motives were to enjoy nature, to educate participants, and to increase environmental sustainability. The important point is that community gardens get started for many reasons, only some of which have to do with producing fresh food.

This last point deserves emphasis. While we are doubtful that home gardening will prove to be the solution to most families' food-insecurity problems, there are many other benefits to gardening that make the activity worthwhile. It is healthier to be in the garden pick-ing aphids off the pepper plants than stretched out on the couch watching television, and if the activity increases one's consumption of healthier foods even a little bit, then so much the better. But when gardening enthusiasts begin to claim that home or community gar-dening can make a significant dent in the larger food-insecurity prob-lem, we think they claim too much.

Despite different purposes, all community gardens are alleged to have similar benefits. They are said to provide opportunities for com-munity members to get physically active, to add some amount of healthy foods to their diet, and to reduce their food costs, if only mar-ginally (Sallis and Glanz 2006; Litt et al. 2011). These benefits and their effects on health have been researched but not very thoroughly (Draper and Freedman 2010). Much of the research is based on com-munity gardens in New York, where the current community garden movement began (Schmelzkopf 1995; Draper and Freedman 2010).

We studied a number of community gardens in and around Orlando. We undertook structured interviews with numerous com-munity gardeners as well as semi-structured, in-depth, open-ended interviews with the leadership of these gardens. (That successful community gardens require leadership is a principal finding from our and other studies, despite the democratic ideals of the alternative-food movement.)

As is almost always the case, the gardens we studied were intended to improve diets, to increase consumption of fresh produce, and to enhance food security. Even so, fewer than two gardeners in five (39 percent) mentioned growing fresh produce as their main personal motivation for getting involved. On average, during harvest periods, our gardeners reported eating something from their garden one to three times a week. One in five reported eating something out of the garden daily; 64 percent of the gardeners said their consumption of fresh vegetables had increased since participating in the community garden.

No one said they ate less fresh produce since they started gardening and many, particularly garden leaders, proudly stated that they already ate healthy, produce-rich diets before their gardening began. A few mentioned the increased enjoyment of eating healthy foods or the cost savings from growing their own. But as the interviews progressed, it became clear that nearly all who had chosen to participate in community gardening *already led a healthy lifestyle and ate a produce-rich diet.* Our impression was that the community gardening movement was to a large extent preaching to the choir. Very few gardeners that we interviewed would qualify as "converts" from unhealthy to healthy food and lifestyle choices.

Physical Activity and Social Capital

Although the gardens we studied did not produce much food (for most, the extra food amounted to a tomato or two here and there), there were other significant benefits that we hasten to acknowledge. Watering and weeding the garden are more healthful activities than watching television or playing video games. Several leaders remarked that their gardeners came mainly for the exercise. Although not strenuous in most cases, gardening at least reduces the time available to be sedentary. Typically, our gardeners visited their gardens a few times a week and stayed for about thirty minutes each visit. Even half an hour of moderate physical activity two or three times a week might have some positive effect on overall well-being.

Many studies (e.g., Ohmer et al. 2009; Mackenzie 2016) also report that community gardening enhances feelings of community and belongingness and extends the gardener's social network. In our study, the average gardener met twelve neighbors they previously did not know. These relationships often entailed conversations while in the garden about mutual interests in living a healthy, sustainable lifestyle. A few gardeners mentioned that these discussions sometimes resulted in friendships that carried beyond the garden, but this was not very prevalent. Interviews with both leaders and gardeners did reveal a sense of community but it was not as strong as some prior studies would lead one to expect, so the main effect was a small increase in one's circle of acquaintances.

Successes and Challenges

With the benefits often ascribed to community gardening by the alternative-food movement, one would expect these gardens to proliferate rapidly and to have many willing participants, but neither of these things is true. Community gardens only succeed when leaders emerge to organize activities, set the rules, and promote participation. They often fail when participation wanes. Thus there was wide consensus among both gardeners and leaders in the Orlando study that the keys to a successful community garden are good leadership and active gardener participation.

Successful community gardens do not magically spring up on abandoned lots in the middle of low-income neighborhoods. The most successful of the many gardens we studied grew out of a community development plan championed by the mayor of Orlando and a city commissioner. The garden was initiated by city government, not by community residents. Proposed in 2005, the garden did not open until 2009—four years to find a proper plot, secure land tenure, thwart opposition (some from the community itself), find people who would take responsibility for making the garden a success, and secure the support of various community leaders. In the years after opening, the garden was kept alive largely by the efforts and energy of a handful of committed women without whose input the garden would have failed. Far from being a spontaneous community-inspired solution to local food-insecurity issues, a successful community garden requires organizational and political skills at least as much as agronomical knowledge.

What is true of leadership skills is also true of gardener participation. It is easy enough to get a few dozen people to show up at an initial meeting to find out what it's all about. It is not so easy to get those people to show up again to clear the lot, or build the beds, or till the soil, or plant and tend the garden. A successful garden requires constant recruitment of new participants and constant efforts to motivate old participants. Without leadership, the garden fails.

Community gardens can indeed have positive impacts on diet, well-being, and community cohesion, but the production of these benefits requires high external inputs—of funds to get a garden going and make needed improvements along the way; of leadership, commitment, and motivation to overcome obstacles and keep the enterprise afloat; and of gardener participation to wrest a reasonable return from the earth. Granted, none of these represent the kinds of external inputs that factory farms require, but they are external inputs nonetheless.

Most of our gardeners reported some increase in their consumption of fresh produce, but realistically these gardens produced only a small to miniscule share of food, even in Florida, which offers two growing seasons a year. At the same time, as an anonymous reviewer put it, while the garden yield "may be small as a percentage of 'money saved' or what shows up on one's plate, . . . it is a start and that is all the alternative-food movement is about." Ostensibly, the alternative-food movement is not about solving the problem of food insecurity or even making much of a dent.

Much of the literature on community gardening is written by advocates, so a close, skeptical reading is necessary, but all the issues that surfaced in our study are widely noted in the literature, although frequently underplayed. The review essay by Guitart, Pickering, and Byrne (2012) concluded that more than half of all papers published on community gardens between 1985 and 2011 discussed challenges that community gardens face.

Sustainable self-provisioning was addressed by a study of home gardeners in Toronto (Kortright and Wakefield 2011). The gardeners in this study generally did not grow enough food to sustain themselves and their families. Nevertheless, approximately one-third of the gardeners did grow a substantial amount of produce. Concerning the limited impact on community cohesion, these authors found that the participants viewed gardening as something that is done for oneself or one's family as opposed to having a larger impact. While the gardeners did share food, they typically shared only small amounts of excess foods. Sharing food was not viewed as a main purpose of the garden. In this Toronto study, "environmental ethics were their central motivation to grow food in their home garden. They value personal action, believe in the importance of eating locally, and feel that it is their duty to use the land they own to grow food" (Kortright and Wakefield 2011:48).

In short, the decision to self-provide through backyard or community gardening is fundamentally ideological, not economic, dietary, or pragmatic. Very few people become engaged in such activities to become self-sufficient in their acquisition of fresh food. For many, the food realized through gardening is the least important aspect of the activity. The Chicago study by Taylor and Lovell (2015) was unable to confirm the hypothesis that urban food gardens successfully lessen household food budgets and could offer only anecdotal evidence that such was the case; the authors also concluded that gardens rely on many external factors that make them difficult to sustain. Donna Armstrong (2000) studied sixty-three community gardens in upstate New York and reported that the majority of these gardens did not hold regular meetings, did not plan cooperative workdays, and did not lead to other community issues being addressed. And yet every one of the studies referenced here concludes with an emphasis on the benefits of community gardening to gardeners and their larger communities.

To be clear, there are important benefits to be realized from backyard and community gardening. As one anonymous reviewer of this chapter put it, "this is a fight worth having." We agree. It is indeed a wonderful thing to wander into the backyard, harvest a plump ripe tomato from the garden, and serve it with the evening salad. But this is a far cry from significantly reducing a household's food insecurity. The value of gardening is more aesthetic or cultural than economic or nutritional.

Guerrilla Gardening

The latest wrinkle in the urban agriculture movement is so-called guerrilla gardening, often described as an act of ecological heroism. A 2013 piece by Rachel Black, herself a guerrilla gardener, touches all the essential themes. It is about how the city of Vancouver came to accept such gardening as a means of promoting its image as an environmentally conscious city in the run-up to the 2010 Winter Olympics.

Ironically, Black was driven into guerrilla gardening because the city's many community gardens all had long waiting lists. The activity is almost always undertaken without permission, because seeking permission would involve negotiating complex bureaucratic channels and might lead to being denied. Thus, gardening becomes ideological and political—"guerrilla warfare" against the urban powers-that-be. It is about contesting and reimagining public space and only coincidentally about growing food.

Guerrilla gardening works best in a supportive, friendly urban environment, which Vancouver was. The city's determination to host the "greenest" Olympics ever made it grateful that abandoned, run-down, weed-infested lots were being replaced by flower and vegetable gardens. Although the gardeners expected resistance, they encountered none. Not all Olympic cities have been as welcoming. "Before the 2006 Winter Olympics in Torino, the City bulldozed a large number of *orti abusive* (illegal gardens) to 'clean up the city' and create spaces for new sports facilities." Illegal gardens hinted at "backwardness and disorder," the exact opposite of the image Torino wanted to present (Black 2013). In the run-up to the Summer Olympics in 2012, London razed a number of community and illegal gardens to make space for sports venues. Gardening and urban agriculture were not part of the image London wanted to present.

Guerrilla gardening is only incidentally about food. Rather, it is about resistance, protest, mobilization, confrontation, community, and contesting. It does not pretend to be about nor does it represent a solution to widespread food insecurity.

Farmers' Markets

If people are unable to grow more of their own food, then perhaps they can at least get closer to those who do. "Farm to table" has become an alluring slogan used by the alternative-food movement, restaurants, and many farmers' markets, and this has led advocates to champion farmers' markets as the next best thing to growing your own food.

Farmers' markets have always existed, of course. Recently, large-scale organized farmers' markets have sprung up in response to the "farm to table" element within the alternative-food movement. According to Liz Grauerholz and Nicole Owens (2015), farmers' markets began to emerge in a big way in the 1970s. In the United States there were 1,755 farmers' markets in 1994; this number increased to 8,144 in 2013 (p. 567). These markets "are supported by consumers who desire greater freshness and quality of products than typically found in stores, hold idealized images of 'local farmers' and less conventional agricultural practices, and who want to help local economies and farmers and feel more connected to their communities" (p. 567).

Many supporters of the alternative-food movement see farmers' markets as a partial antidote to food insecurity, and there is now a federal program encouraging farmers' markets to accept SNAP cards. Congress has provided expanded eligibility for USDA grants to improve access to fresh produce and healthy foods by SNAP recipients at farmers' markets. There is also a Farmers Market Nutrition Program (FMNP) inside the Women, Infants, and Children program. One of the WIC's aim is to provide nutritious food to eligible people, which includes pregnant, postpartum, and breastfeeding women, and infants and children younger than five years of age who are deemed nutritionally at risk. In many states, like Florida, WIC funds cannot be used to purchase produce at farmers' markets. The FMNP is an incentive program to allow farmers' markets to accept WIC-FMNP coupons as payment (Owens and Donley 2015). As these two examples make clear, the federal government believes that low-income families are nutritionally better off shopping at farmers' markets than at conventional grocery stores.

There are many different kinds of farmers' markets, so generalization is difficult. Despite the imagery of locally sourced food, many farmers' markets place no restrictions on the origins of the produce being vended. More and more, however, these markets do restrict sellers to food grown within some specific radius—a hundred miles seems to be the most usual arrangement.

It is also not true that farmers' markets convey produce directly from farmers to consumers. Many of the vendors are not farmers at all but resellers who buy food either from farmers or from wholesale warehouses and then resell it. Farmers' markets often do not allow consumers to "look the farmer in the eye." Managers of farmers' markets themselves believe that their markets are part of the solution to food insecurity, or should be. Julie Guthman, Amy Morris, and Patricia Allen (2006) found that 81 percent of managers of farmers' markets in California believed that it is important to address food security through such markets, despite their simultaneous perception that more than 90 percent of their customers are either middle- or high-income consumers.

A recent study (Lucan et al. 2015) has raised doubts about the convenience, accessibility, quality, variety, price, and overall superiority of farmers' markets compared to regular supermarkets as places for families to purchase food. The study design was simple. All known farmers' markets in Bronx County, New York (twenty-six), and one (or two) of the nearest full-service supermarkets selling fresh produce (forty-four stores) were selected for the study. Researchers were then sent to each farmers' market and each supermarket to record variables related to accessibility (nearness to one another, hours of operation); variety (number and types of food and fresh produce offered in each store); quality (where produce was grown, whether it was grown organically); and price (factoring in sales and promotions). The results were stunning.

The mean distance between farmers' markets and the nearest store selling fresh produce was 0.15 miles (range of 0.02–0.36 miles). Farmers' markets were open substantially fewer months, days, and hours than supermarkets. Farmers' markets offered 26.4 fewer fresh produce items on average than stores. Produce items at farmers' markets were more frequently local and organic, but often tended toward less common or more exotic and heirloom varieties. Farmers' markets were more expensive on average—even for more commonplace and "conventional" produce—especially when discounts or sales prices were considered. A third (32.8 percent) of what farmers' markets offered was not fresh produce at all but refined or processed products (e.g., jams, pies, cakes, cookies, donuts, juice drinks). Thus, farmers' markets may offer many items not optimal for good nutrition and health and may carry less varied, less common fresh produce in neighborhoods that already have access to stores with cheaper prices and overwhelmingly more hours of operation.

One commentator on the study (Jacobs 2015) remarked that farmers' markets "are basically boutiques, offering produce that is more exotic, and more expensive, than the grocery stores located nearby. What's more, their merchandise includes many items not optimal for good health." Jacobs does acknowledge that the produce at farmers' markets is somewhat fresher and more likely to be organic, but cites another study (Smith-Spangler et al. 2012) that raises doubts whether so-called organic food is in fact any healthier than conventionally grown food. Sean Lucan and colleagues (2015) concluded that farmers' markets do not seem to improve the urban food environment very much, if at all. Tom Jacobs (2015) comments: "Sure, they're a great place to mingle. But as to whether they are a net nutritional plus for the neighborhood, the answer appears to be: Not so much."

Class, Race, Food Sovereignty, and Food Insecurity

In enumerating the challenges and considerations currently being faced by the alternative-food movement, Grauerholz and Owens remark that the ability of the alternative-food movements "to address issues of equity, food security, class, gender, and race" (2015:570) is problematic. The basic issue is that food insecurity is a poverty issue, whereas the alternative-food movement appeals mainly to affluent middle-class whites. "Many involved in food movements emphasize educating people which can result in 'telling others what to eat,' rather than focusing on access, affordability, and structural inequality that make [alternative-food movements] unsustainable and difficult to develop" (p. 570). Or as Julie Guthman (2011) describes it in the title of her paper, the problem is "the unbearable whiteness of alternative food."

Guthman's essay is a spirited data-based attack on the inability or unwillingness of alternate-food enthusiasts to speak intelligently to the low-income, nonwhite community, a problem that many advocates acknowledge but quickly dismiss as a mere educational issue. "If people only knew" where their food comes from, they would be much more accepting of alternatives—locally grown food, farm-to-table food, backyard and community gardening, farmers' markets, and all the rest. Guthman raises questions about this central metaphor of the alternative-food movement: "Who is the speaker? How do we identify those who do not know the source of their food? What would they do if they did know? Do they not know now?" (2011:263).

The essence of Guthman's argument is that "many of the discourses of alternative food hail a white subject and thereby code the practices and spaces of alternative food as white" (p. 264). This, she adds, has a "chilling effect" on nonwhite people and therefore functions as an exclusionary principle. Simply put, poor, nonwhite people do not participate in the alternative-food movement because they are conscious of the "whiteness" of the spaces of the movement (markets, gardens, and community events).

A key element of the "whiteness" of the alternative-food movement is "universalism: the assumption that values held primarily by whites are normal and widely shared" (p. 267). With this assumption comes a refusal "to acknowledge the experience, aesthetics, and ideals of others, with the pernicious effect that those who do not conform to white ideals are justifiably marginalized" (p. 268). Inside the alternative-food movement, the superiority of healthy, local, sustainable eating is assumed, and those who do not share the assumption have simply made "bad lifestyle choices" and need proper education. In short, they embrace inferior values and need reform. That what one eats is not necessarily a "choice" in low-income and ethnic communities is never considered, and the ramifications are rarely appreciated.

Another element of the race-class conundrum is that the imagery of the alternative-food movement evokes different images of the agrarian past for different races and classes (a point made by Guthman with particular eloquence). Middle-class whites may romanticize the rural past—the imagined, almost mythical era of the family farm where everyone understood where their food came from and lived in close harmony with the natural world. People who are closer to the rural past, however, may have heard from their parents and grandparents that the family farm was a locus of back-breaking dawn-to-dusk labor for half the year; that drought, insects, and other uncontrollable variables could wipe out an entire season of labor; and that half a year of eating potatoes morning, noon, and night because all the other crops failed was not particularly fun. Finally, to the African American population, the rural past evokes the imagery of slave society. For them, "putting your hands in the dirt" evokes bitter memories, not fond nostalgia. (On race and the alternative-food movement, see also Alkon 2012; Bowens 2015.)

Many of these points have been made by Yuki Kato (2013) in her study of community-supported agriculture in post-Katrina New Orleans. Kato's concern was the lack of participation in community-supported agriculture by local residents, the vast bulk of whom were low-income African Americans. She distinguishes between food access and food sovereignty, explaining that food access refers to the production and distribution of healthy food, while food sovereignty refers to efforts to control ownership of the food system. Both are essential to what the alternative-food movement calls "food justice," but Kato's analysis suggests that the community-supported agriculture she studied accomplished neither.

Kato studied an urban community-supported agriculture market in the Hollygrove neighborhood of New Orleans, a city that has witnessed a proliferation of urban agriculture since the devastation of Katrina. The community-supported agriculture organization itself was a produce reseller: it would purchase mostly locally grown produce from within a seventy-mile radius then sell the produce at the community-supported agriculture market. A total of 147 consumers of this community-supported agriculture market were surveyed, and some thirty in-depth interviews were conducted. Of the 147 customers surveyed, fewer than 4 percent lived in the Hollygrove neighborhood, so the research question was why people in the neighborhood did not participate in the community-supported agriculture despite outreach, financial incentives, and other inducements. The research uncovered three forms of constraint: economic, sociocultural, and spatial.

The economic constraint was that market produce was too expensive for local residents to afford. As for the sociocultural constraints, there were major differences between what community-supported agriculture enthusiasts thought and what local residents said. Consistent with Guthman's (2011) study, supporters of community-supported agriculture felt that lack of knowledge was a key explanation. That is, people in the neighborhood did not understand the superior nutritional value or taste of locally grown food; did not know how to prepare fresh food; were intimidated by the exotic, nonstandard offerings (bok choy and "all these crazy things they've never heard of"); and did not comprehend the damage inflicted on the environment by industrial farming.

As for customers, the biggest complaint was the price, and the second biggest complaint was that the community-supported agriculture market did not sell the products they wanted to buy. Onions, green peppers, and celery constitute the "holy trinity" of New Orleans cooking, but when customers asked for these items, they were told that they would be available only "in season." So the produce in the market did not respect the culinary traditions of the neighborhood.

The Hollygrove community-supported agriculture market catered to a food-focused, well-educated, affluent, white, upper-middle-class clientele, not to the low-income African American residents of the neighborhood. In the end, the community-supported agriculture operation failed to garner much support from the local community and never found an effective food justice narrative that resonated with the Hollygrove community. The managers of the community-supported agriculture market forgot that food carries cultural identity and that when people are told they need to change what and how they eat, some piece of their cultural identity gets chipped away and discarded. Food insecurity is unequal access to food, and unequal access to food, just like unequal access to housing, education, and health care, has been shaped by racial inequality and residential segregation.

Nicholas Larchet (2014) studied a community-supported agriculture program and a farmers' market in a large southeastern US city and found exactly the same processes. Both programs were located in underserved communities but failed to attract a poor, black clientele. Most of the people in the farmers' market and most participants in the community-supported agriculture program were white, middle-class professionals.

Does the alternative-food movement represent a potential solution to food insecurity? We cede the conclusion to Grauerholz and Owens: "It is unlikely that families can survive on local yield alone, thus local foods are likely to supplement rather than replace conventional food production and consumption" (2015:568).

Food Banks and Food Pantries

If people can't really grow much of their own food and lack the money to buy the food they need, what's left? For many low-income food-insecure households, the answer is the vast array of food banks and food pantries operating across the nation. Are the food pantries a new form of food sovereignty among the poor? Do they provide a new entitlement to food? Do they represent a plausible solution to the underlying problem?

The Gospel according to Matthew 25:35–40 (beginning, "For I was hungry and you gave me something to eat, I was thirsty and you gave me something to drink") has defined the Christian social obligation for two millennia, and much of the effort to feed the needy has come from faith-based organizations. For example, there are more than 600 food pantries associated with the Second Harvest Food Bank of Central Florida, and over 80 percent of them are affiliated with faith-based organizations. The same is presumably true nationwide.

Our research group at the University of Central Florida has studied the food pantry system and its clients in the area for more than a decade. The pantry system of emergency food distribution probably offers the best hope for resolving food insecurity (unless we can find a way to redistribute income), because the pantries and the food banks that support them have the means and will to provide food to food-insecure people. But this is not to say that the pantry system is without problems. On the contrary, we have observed many issues with the pantry system that limit its effectiveness in resolving the problem.

Where the Need Is and the Food Isn't

Most communities in the United States have one or more emergency food pantries where people in need can go to obtain food. These pantries are sometimes described as the first line of defense against hunger. The website www.foodpantries.org lists 15,124 known food pantries in the United States, and this listing is bound to be incomplete. Pantries are distinct from soup kitchens, where people in need go to eat prepared meals, and also distinct from the food banks, which are suppliers of food to the food pantries.

Although food pantries are ubiquitous, large percentages of poor and food-insecure people are unaware of a church, food pantry, or food bank in their neighborhood where they could get emergency food if in need. About half of the food-insecure know of such places but the other half do not. Already, the pantries do not address half of the overall problem. A second concern is less with unawareness than with the spatial ecology of the pantry system—whether the system adequately covers the areas of greatest need. The pantries have to be located somewhere, typically in or near the main site of the sponsoring organization, but how does the spatial distribution of the pantries stack up against the geography of need?

We compiled data on need for food and amounts of food delivered to all census tracts in Brevard, Lake, Orange, Osceola, Seminole, and Volusia counties in Central Florida. (Orange, Lake, Osceola, and Seminole counties define the Orlando metro area.) We used census and community indicators to identify the relative need for food across 613 census tracts in the six-county region. Second Harvest Food Bank contributed data on the location of food outlets and the amount of food they delivered to the outlets in every tract.

Analyses showed that all indicators of need (poverty rate, total population, percentage nonwhite, number of food stamp households, etc.) were positively correlated with the amount of food delivered to a tract—obviously an encouraging result. But none of the correlations was perfect, so despite the general tendency of emergency food to go where need is greatest, there is still the possibility of slippage between need and system response. To explore this possibility, we used a simple regression equation to calculate how much food a census tract *should* receive given its population, poverty rate, and other need indicators, compared that prediction with how much food it actually received, and then examined cases where the discrepancy was greatest. (Readers with statistical training will recognize this as an analysis of the regression residuals.) By customary standards, the model fit the data moderately well.

The analysis of residuals identified twenty-seven census tracts in the six-county area whose estimated food shortfall exceeded 100,000 pounds, ten of them in Orange County. All twenty-seven have existing food pantries, but residents in these tracts need more food assistance than they currently receive. Importantly, these tracts were *not* located in dense, inner-city, high-poverty areas as we expected, but rather in the more isolated, rural, outlying areas, especially in areas with relatively high proportions of seniors.

There are many reasons why food pantries are situated where they are. Most pantries are near the churches, synagogues, and mosques that sponsor them. This ecological pattern favors densely populated areas at the expense of sparsely settled places—cities are well-served while the rural areas suffer. There is also evidence that local poverty conditions dictate pantry locations more than local demographic conditions, such as a high percentage of elderly. So there are certain readily observed inefficiencies in where the pantries are located. The food pantries are not always available in the areas of greatest need.

Insufficiencies of Supply

Many "gap" studies have been done, usually at the level of whole counties, and nearly all conclude that the most serious gap involves the sheer quantity of food available for distribution. Most food pantries apparently need to increase the availability of food by providing more food and more options to more clients more frequently. When we interview food pantry patrons in Central Florida, the most common complaint is that the amount of food they are allowed to take is not sufficient. Pantry operators generally define their mission as "supplemental" and most have elaborate regulations on how often families can receive food and how much food families can receive (are entitled to?). They often do not acknowledge that many of their clients depend almost entirely on pantry food, not as "supplemental" but as their main source of nutrition. Many patrons find it necessary to "shop" at multiple pantries to ensure their families have a sufficient supply of food.

Problems with Access

Increasing access is the key to eliminating gaps in the emergency food distribution system. Several access issues are raised in the literature. The first regards hours of operation; food outlets need to be open on days and times when clients can access them but frequently are not. This is a disturbingly common problem. Second, services are not adequately publicized. Outreach to the most vulnerable populations is essential. Third, there is a need to increase clients' knowledge of nutrition and food preparation. In the modern era, just feeding the poor and hungry is not enough. Food pantries need to be concerned with health and nutrition when providing food to clients, just as school nutritionists are when planning weekly meal plans. And yet end-users of food distribution systems are often found to lack information on issues of nutrition, food preparation, healthy eating, and the like. The fourth issue concerns service areas: food pantries can improve access by increasing the number of sites where food is distributed and reducing miles between sites where possible. Fifth and finally, there are larger systemic issues, in that food banks are forced to pursue incompatible and even contradictory goals, namely to work as hard as they can to feed the hungry while at the same time working toward a more just society where people can afford to feed themselves. Food is not the problem. As we have stressed repeatedly, poverty is the problem. But if food banks used up their resources fighting poverty, little or nothing would be left to feed hungry people.

Accessibility of Food Outlets by Public Transportation

We obtained data on food pantry locations from Second Harvest Food Bank in two counties (Orange and Seminole) where the local public transportation system (Lynx) provides service. We then used ArcGIS, a geographic information system, to map locations of Lynx bus stops against food pantry locations in those two counties. We determined if any Lynx bus stops were present within one-quarter mile of each pantry location. In general, food outlets located in the central urbanized core are mostly accessible by bus, but this is generally not true of the pantries in the suburban regions. In Seminole County and in the more suburbanized regions of Orange County, people can access the food distribution system only if they have access to a car or happen to live within biking or walking distance.

Accessibility of Information

The physical accessibility of a food outlet, while critical, is no more important than the accessibility of information about days and times when the outlet is open, rules about how often clients can come, and related information. As our studies progressed, we were taken aback by how difficult it was for us to make contact with, or obtain any information about, the food outlets we wanted to study. Phone calls would regularly go unanswered, or were answered by a voice mail message that imparted nothing we needed to know (where are you located, when are you open?). In one afternoon, we called every Second Harvest Food Bank food outlet in Seminole County that was on the list we had been given, about thirty pantries. Only two of these calls were answered by a human, and in neither of these cases was the human we talked to able to answer our questions. We had similar although somewhat less extreme experiences trying to contact the food outlets in Orange and Osceola counties as well.

Why Food Pantries Are Not the Solution

The takeaway from this discussion is that the network of food banks, soup kitchens, and food pantries, although well-intentioned, mainly addresses the symptoms of food insecurity, not the underlying causes. Not to quarrel with the New Testament, but the passage from Matthew seems to suggest that the solution to food insecurity and hunger is to be found in individual acts of charity, not in systemic policy changes. But as actor Jeff Bridges (2010) has rightly noted:

> Public charities, food banks and church pantries are doing more than ever before, but they can't keep up with the need. We can never end hunger only through the wonderful work of local charities. Like other Western democracies, we must end our national problem of hunger through national and political leadership. Charity is nice for some things, but not as a way to feed a nation. We don't protect our national security through charity, and we shouldn't protect our families and children that way either.

Conclusions

We can conclude from the evidence reviewed in this chapter that it is not realistic to expect food-insecure people to farm or garden themselves out of their food-insecure condition, and it is equally unrealistic to expect private charities, churches, food pantries, and food banks to solve the problem. This leaves public policy as the solution of last resort, the topic of the next chapter.

6

The Public Policy Connection

As we noted in the preceding chapter, charity is no way to feed a nation. In fact, all modern societies have evolved public policy measures to reduce food insecurity among various population subgroups. Here we discuss three large federal feeding programs in the United States: Meals on Wheels, targeted to seniors; the school breakfast and lunch program, targeted to low-income children; and SNAP, targeted to the poor. All make a definite and positive contribution to food security and better nutrition in their target audiences but face serious issues of under-utilization that limit their effectiveness.

Meals on Wheels

One of the most successful meal programs ever implemented is Meals on Wheels, which originated in the United Kingdom in 1943 during the German Blitz. The idea of delivering meals to persons unable to prepare their own meals evolved into modern-day programs targeted mainly to frail, homebound elders. The first home-delivered-meal program in the United States was in Philadelphia in 1954, followed quickly by similar programs in Columbus, Ohio, and Rochester, New York. Today, there are Meals on Wheels programs in all fifty states, throughout Canada and Australia, and in most of Europe as well. The total number of these programs in just the United States numbers in the tens of thousands.

There is a great deal of local autonomy in how specific Meals on Wheels programs operate, the services they offer, eligibility restrictions, what meals are delivered, and whether there are provisions for special dietary needs. Some programs deliver two meals a day; most only serve lunch.[1] Most restrict deliveries to Monday through Friday. Some allow for special dietary needs, some sponsor congregate feeding programs,[2] but others do not. Many programs are not even called "Meals on Wheels" but go by other names. All restrict services to persons aged sixty and older (this by virtue of the federal Older Americans Act [OAA], which helps fund these programs) and virtually all rely on volunteers to get meals delivered. Meals on Wheels programs also provide socialization and some degree of safety checking along with meals. Thus, the frequent motto is "more than just a meal."

One controversial aspect of the program is that there is not supposed to be any means-testing. The federal OAA officially does not allow it. "However, while there is no means test for participation in the OAA Nutrition Programs, services are targeted to older adults with the greatest social and/or economic need with particular attention to low-income minorities" (Older Americans Act 2002). In practice (in most agencies), the "no means test" provision means that no client is denied service because of inability to pay, but many Meals on Wheels programs have a sliding fee based on clients' income, and programs without a fee system encourage donations. In a national study of program participants (Ponza, Ohls, and Millen 1996), 94 percent of congregate-meal participants and 73 percent of home-delivered-meal participants said they usually made a contribution.

Meals on Wheels is a benefit partly funded under the OAA, not an entitlement. The program is not intended to feed all seniors who would otherwise be food-insecure. Nor is the reduction of food insecurity among seniors the primary goal. The principal goal is to provide meals to people who are unable to prepare their own meals so they can "age in place." But according to the Administration on Aging, "The OAA Nutrition Program targets services to vulnerable older adults who are older, poorer, sicker, at higher nutritional risk, more functionally impaired, more likely to live alone, and more likely to be a minority member than the general U.S. population" (Older Americans Act 2002:5).

What It Costs

In recent years, total federal funding for the Elderly Nutrition Services (ENS) Program of the OAA, which includes both home-delivered and congregate meals, has hovered near $1 billion annually, and that money is used to provide about 250 million meals to about 2.6 million people. Only about half of the total cost is borne by the federal government; the remainder comes from client fees, churches, grants, foundations, and local donors. Empirically, the average true dollar cost in 2009 for a congregate meal was $6.96, and $5.30 for a home-delivered meal (Colello 2011). (About three-fifths of the ENS funding goes to home-delivered meals, the remainder to congregate feedings.) Because of the increase in the number of frail elderly, the number of home-delivered meals served has increased more rapidly than the number of congregate meals.

Estimates of the percentage of food-insecure, frail, and needy seniors who participate in Meals on Wheels or associated congregate feeding programs range from as few as a tenth to as many as a quarter. Either way, the large majority are uncovered. Most Meals on Wheels programs maintain a waiting list that is often as long as the number of clients served. Meals on Wheels is not intended to eliminate food insecurity among seniors, so the shortfall in coverage would be scarcely worth mentioning except that Meals on Wheels is often assumed to be "taking care" of the senior end of the food-insecurity problem—an incorrect assumption.

Evidence of Success

According to Kirsten Colello (2011), "The [Meals on Wheels] program is designed to address problems of food insecurity, promote socialization, and promote the health and well-being of older persons through nutrition and nutrition-related services." Whether Meals on Wheels accomplishes these things is a research question, and "nutritional research on the OAA Nutrition Program, our nation's largest food and nutrition assistance program specifically targeted to older adults, is relatively sparse" (Wellman 2010:1151). Another research team has also noted the surprising absence of research on this topic (Payette and Shatenstein 2005). The last comprehensive evaluation was conducted by Mathematica Policy Research in 1996 (Ponza, Ohls, and Millen 1996) and is thus more than twenty years out-of-date. But it's the best study we have.

The report covers a large number of topics (funding, program administration, relationships with other programs, and service delivery issues), but the ones most relevant to our concerns are program participation and program impacts. The health status of program participants underscores their vulnerability and disability. About half report three or more chronic physical health conditions. As would be expected, recipients of home-delivered meals are sicker than congregate-meal participants, often by large margins. About half of all participants take three or more medications daily. A third of congregant meal participants and two-thirds of home-delivered-meal participants rate their overall health as only fair or poor. Functional status is also highly compromised. Among home-delivered-meal participants, 77 percent are either unable to perform or have great difficulty performing one or more activities of daily living.[3] Among the home-delivered-meal group, the majority (54 percent) never leave their homes and only 15 percent get out of the house five or more times weekly.

Participants in both home-delivered and congregate-meal programs are much more likely to experience food insecurity compared to the general senior population. Further, a significant number of participants fail to get the Recommended Daily Allowance (RDA) of nutrients. Thus, while most program clients are properly fed, significantly large minorities are not.

Consistent with published standards, the lunches *as served* provide approximately one-third of the RDA stipulations for most nutrients (the design standard). Important issues remain. An analysis of total diets (the Meals on Wheels meals plus whatever else participants consumed) showed that among participants in congregate and home-delivered-meal programs, the average intake from program meals was between 36 and 51 percent of their total daily intake of eighteen nutrients examined (Ponza, Ohls, and Millen 1996:106). Because the program meal should contribute one-third of each nutrient but in fact contributes more than a third of every nutrient and in some cases over half, the implication is that participants' other daily meals (breakfast and dinner in most cases) are nutritionally deficient. Qualitative studies also suggest considerable hoarding of the program meal; some is eaten for lunch as intended, but some is saved to be eaten later. The general issue is that most people, including most Meals on Wheels participants, eat three meals a day, or twenty-one meals a week, of which only five (typically) are program meals.

A complicated multivariate statistical analysis reported in the Mathematica evaluation compared nutrient intakes of program participants with nutrient intakes of equally low-income nonparticipants, holding constant confounding factors. The average nutrient intakes for those eating in congregate-meal programs are higher than for those not eating at such meal programs, often 10 to 20 percent higher. The study also found statistically significant differences in the mean nutrient intake among congregate-meal participants versus nonparticipants for sixteen of the eighteen nutrients studied. The results were broadly similar for the home-delivered-meal group. Other studies also show dietary or nutritional improvements among Meals on Wheels participants (Keller 2006; Roy and Payette 2006; Frongillo et al. 2010; Frongillo and Wolfe 2010; Greenlee 2011). But Kathy Greenlee (2011) reports (somewhat ominously) that 63 percent of his study subjects relied on their home-delivered meal for half or more of their total food.

That participants are better off nutritionally than nonparticipants is confirmed in a recent review of relevant literature on the topic (Zhu and Ruopeng 2013). These authors identified eight studies that met their quality, sampling, and design criteria. Six of the eight studies found that home-delivered-meal programs led to improved diet quality, increased nutrient intakes, and reduced food insecurity among participants. They also found increased levels of socialization opportunities, improvements in dietary adherence, and an overall higher quality of life.

Another issue is "meal utilization"—how much and what of the delivered meal is consumed. One study showed that on average, only 81 percent of the energy content of the meal was consumed; the other 19 percent was wasted (Fogler-Levitt et al. 1995). Food is wasted for many reasons, including participants not liking a particular food, food having a disagreeable texture, and unfamiliarity with specific foods (Krassie, Smart, and Roberts 2000).

In summary, Meals on Wheels and the associated congregate feeding reach the populations they were intended to reach, are hugely popular with recipients, make a measurable difference in the nutritional status of recipients, promote socialization, keep mobility-limited persons in their homes and out of institutions, and increase physical, mental, and social well-being among vulnerable seniors. What more could one ask of any social program, most of all a program that costs the federal government only a billion or so dollars a year?

The Waiting Lists and Coverage and Outreach

Yet important issues remain, chief among them the long waiting lists and the large unaddressed needs. We conducted a small study of how Orange County seniors on Meals on Wheels waiting lists managed to feed themselves and the portrait was generally grim (Gualtieri et al. 2018). Seniors on Meals on Wheels waiting lists, particularly those with high needs-assessment scores, are in serious need of food assistance. It is frustrating that people on these waiting lists have already been identified as food-insecure; their locations and contact information are known; and their need for assistance is obvious. Yet still they wait.

Most Meals on Wheels programs do target resources to their priority clients in that the clients served are mostly poor, food-insecure, aged, and mobility-restricted. At the same time, most seniors (three-quarters or more) in need do not receive Meals on Wheels resources. What accounts for who makes it into a Meals on Wheels program and who does not?

Priority scores matter, but less than one might think. In jurisdictions where demand greatly exceeds supply (about 70 percent of all jurisdictions), Meals on Wheels may never even clear all the high-priority cases. Low-priority clients can therefore languish on the waiting list for years. A second factor is whether potential clients live within the delivery area of Meals on Wheels.

Do Meals on Wheels programs offer any sort of systematic outreach to identify clients in need? According to Jung Lee and colleagues (2008), the answer is yes, but not much. A national phone survey of twenty-nine Area Agency on Aging (AAA) directors and sixty-four local Meals on Wheels providers revealed that only about 10 percent reported "little or no outreach." However, one in four listed "word of mouth" as a local outreach strategy, which seems a bit of a stretch (even though word of mouth is often effective). Then there were agency newsletters, speaking engagements, health fairs and awareness events, media spots, and hospital, church, and senior center postings. Not one mention was made by any respondent of direct, proactive efforts to identify dense clusters of seniors or of door-to-door canvassing to identify those in need.

Adequacy of the Food Served

Most Meals on Wheels programs serve only lunch, and the federal standards require that these lunches provide at least 30 percent of all dietary intake necessary for good health. And yet we know empirically that on average, these lunches constitute about half of participants' total daily dietary intake, at least for most nutrients and the majority of clients. The Meals on Wheels lunch could be fortified to contain more nutrients, but with significant cost implications. The policy question then becomes whether we want to save money or enhance the quality of life for our seniors?

In the end, Meals on Wheels is to senior food insecurity what Habitat for Humanity is to homelessness. Within the confines of programmatic intent and current funding levels, these are wonderful programs fully deserving of public and private support. But in both cases, the numbers are such that making a measurable dent in the larger problem is just not in the cards unless available resources are sharply increased.

Free and Reduced-Cost School Breakfast and Lunch Programs

If one were to ask what provisions the federal government has made to address food insecurity among children in America's low-income families, the most obvious answer would be the free and reduced-cost breakfast and lunch programs in the nation's public schools.[4] Indeed, these programs are second only to SNAP (among feeding programs) in their drawdown on the federal budget and are now running at an annual cost of $15–16 billion. (Annual SNAP costs are in the vicinity of $80 billion.) The question is whether these programs improve the nutritional status of low-income students.

School breakfasts and lunches have been available to American elementary, middle, and secondary school students for decades. The National School Lunch Program (NSLP) is the older of two programs, having been created in 1946. To date, the NSLP has served more than 224 billion lunches (US Department of Agriculture 2015a). The School Breakfast Program (SBP) came much later in 1975 (US Department of Agriculture 2015b). The SBP has seen a steady increase in student participation over the years, with 1.8 million children served daily in 1975 up to 12.1 million served daily in 2011, more than a sixfold increase (US Department of Agriculture 2012). Both programs are federally subsidized and administered by the US Department of Agriculture.

Federal funding helps ensure that the cost of school meals is not prohibitive, particularly for low- and moderate-income families. Any child who attends a school that participates in the NSLP or the SBP (or both) may purchase a meal. What they are asked to pay for the meal is determined by family income (Food Research and Action Center 2015). Children whose family incomes fall between 130 and 185 percent of the federal poverty level are eligible for reduced-cost school meals. If family income is less than 130 percent of the poverty level, children are qualified to receive free meals under both programs. During the 2013–2014 school year, 130 percent of the poverty level was $30,615 for a family of four, and 185 percent of the poverty level was $43,568 (US Department of Agriculture 2014). The free and reduced-price (FRP) school meals are intended to guarantee that all school children have access to one (or two) nutritionally balanced meals on every school day.

To be eligible for FRP meals, a child must be "certified." A child can be certified by completing a paper application indicating family income and need, but this is not always required. Schools can directly certify students whose life circumstances make them automatically qualified. "Categorically eligible" students are those already enrolled in other programs such as foster care or Head Start, those who come from migrant or homeless families, and those whose families receive familial benefits such as SNAP, Temporary Assistance to Needy Families (TANF), or Food Distribution Program on Indian Reservations (FDPIR) (Food Research and Action Center 2015).

Additional measures to increase participation are in place. The community eligibility provision (CEP) was introduced in 2010 to permit school districts to offer universal free breakfast and lunch if the students who are automatically certified constitute at least 40 percent of the total school population (Food Research and Action Center 2015). In this manner, all students in schools with a high percentage of low-income children have access to free meals without the need to complete paper applications and track types of meals served (full-price or FRP). Schools are reimbursed using a formula based on the number of children automatically certified.

An additional measure is "Provision 2," under which schools in which at least 75 percent of their students are low-income only have to collect applications and track meals (paid or FRP) once every four years to receive federal reimbursements (US Department of Agriculture 2014). This provision is intended to save labor costs and provide universal free meals. Both the CEP and Provision 2 address key barriers to participation in the SBP and the NSLP by reducing student wait time in the cafeteria and by reducing the stigma associated with accepting a free meal.

There have always been strict nutritional guidelines for both programs. Participants must be served so much of this and so much of that, and only meals that meet these guidelines are eligible for federal reimbursement. Cafeteria workers therefore staff end-of-line stations to ensure that each tray qualifies for reimbursement. Students are often told, "You need a carton of milk" or "Go back and get a serving of veggies" and soon incorporate these requirements into their cafeteria-line behavior.

The US Department of Agriculture (2015a) estimates that, on average, 30.4 million children participated each day in the NSLP in fiscal year 2014 and that over two-thirds of the 5 billion lunches served were FRP. During the same period, an estimated 13.6 million children participated in the SBP, and of the 2.3 billion breakfasts served, 85 percent were FRP (US Department of Agriculture 2015b).

A significant issue with both programs since inception is that reimbursements are made on the basis of food *served,* regardless of whether those meals are eaten in full, in part, or not at all. This is the much discussed problem of "plate waste" that we take up later.

Over time, there has been a steady increase in the number of participants receiving an FRP meal. In 1969, 15 percent of the total lunches served in the NSLP were FRP. In marked contrast, 72 percent of the lunches served in 2014 were FRP (US Department of Agriculture 2015b). Similarly, in the SBP, the percentage of total breakfast meals that are FRP has fluctuated from year to year, but ultimately increased from 76.3 percent in 1971 to 84.9 percent in 2014 (US Department of Agriculture 2015b). Thus, over time, school meal programs have come to rely more and more heavily on the federal reimbursement. In the Orange County public school system, for example, virtually 100 percent of the food and nutrition budget is obtained via the federal reimbursement.

The Problem

With the kinds of numbers these school meal programs generate, one might think that at least this part of the overall food-insecurity problem is solved, but as an effort to eliminate hunger among school-aged children, the SBP and NSLP have widely acknowledged problems. To begin, these programs provide two meals a day, but children need three; they provide meals on school days, but children need to eat on weekends and holidays; they operate when schools are in session, but children also need to eat when school is not in session. Many local food banks and pantries attempt to fill in these gaps with various after-school and summer feeding programs, with greater or lesser success.

Setting aside issues with evenings, weekends, holidays, and summers, and despite the millions of meals served annually, there are still concerns. A big one is that many students do not participate in the program even when they are eligible to do so. Philip Gleason (1995) noted over two decades ago that a significant number of students who were eligible for FRP meals did not actually participate. Elementary and middle school students tend to participate in the SBP and NSLP in fairly large numbers, but participation falls by half for secondary school students (see also Castillo and Lofton 2012). Lack of participation obviously limits the effectiveness of the FRP meal programs in addressing the food problems of the young.

A related concern is that participating in school meal programs does not necessarily equate to minimally adequate food consumption. Research has documented large amounts of plate waste by those who accept FRP meals (Haas, Cunningham-Sabo, and Auld 2014; Smith and Cunningham-Sabo 2013). These two factors—participation and plate waste—combine to reduce the effectiveness of FRP school meal programs in ensuring a nutritionally adequate diet for children, particularly adolescents, from low- and moderate-income families (Hakim and Meissen 2013).

Determinants of Participation

What factors are associated with participation in the school meal programs? Males are more likely than females to eat a school lunch or breakfast (Gleason 1995; Mirtcheva and Powell 2009), and females are more likely to skip breakfast than males, regardless of food-security status (Potamites and Gordon 2010). Females also have more plate waste than males (Marlette, Templeton, and Panemangalore 2005; Haas, Cunningham-Sabo, and Auld 2014). Geographic location also matters. As Gleason (1995) notes, students in rural locations are more likely to participate in the NSLP than are those living in urban districts. Minority students have a greater rate of participation than white students (Gleason 1995; Newman and Ralston 2006; Mirtcheva and Powell 2009). Additionally, lower family income (less than 185 percent of the poverty line) results in greater participation rates (Gleason 1995; Potamites and Gordon 2010).

Demographics aside, we know quite a bit about why students do or do not eat school meals. Food quality is the most important factor (Asperin, Nettles, and Carr 2008; Castillo and Lofton 2012; Cohen et al. 2013; Smith and Cunningham-Sabo 2013). Food quality includes appearance, aroma, nutritional value, freshness, and overall taste (Roseman and Niblock 2006; Castillo and Lofton 2012; Bailey-Davis et al. 2013). Using a nationally representative sample of over 3,000 students, Gleason (1995) found that the main reason students did not eat the school lunch is that they did not like the food they were offered. More recent studies find the same thing (Castillo, Lofton, and Nettles 2011; Castillo and Lofton 2012; Bailey-Davis et al. 2013).

With this documented dislike of food quality, the past decade or so has witnessed more and more studies of plate waste (Marlette, Templeton, and Panemangalore 2005; Cohen et al. 2013; Smith and Cunningham-Sabo 2013) and actual consumption (Swanson 2008). Although vast amounts of food are served to America's schoolchildren, a significant portion of it goes into cafeteria waste bins. Interestingly, there is no significant difference between the plate waste of students who are food-secure and those who are food-insecure (Potamites and Gordon 2010). In other words, hungry children are no more likely to consume food they do not like than anyone else. Poor food quality has been found to discourage participation and consumption in both the breakfast (Bailey-Davis et al. 2013) and lunch (Castillo and Lofton 2012) programs. Students self-report that they throw out, on average, 25 percent of their school lunches, most often because of taste (Castillo, Lofton, and Nettles 2011; Haas, Cunningham-Sabo, and Auld 2014).

Although low food quality is the number one reason kids don't eat school meals, time is another issue. Rushed morning schedules at home, late buses, slow entry into school due to security measures, and the desire to socialize instead of eat breakfast all serve as barriers to a student's participation in the SBP (Florida Impact 2014). Parents and their middle school students also note that oversleeping is a common reason for missing or skipping breakfast, both at home and at school (Bailey-Davis et al. 2013). School systems across the nation have attempted to deal with this by offering breakfast foods outside the cafeteria through a "grab and go" brown bag option (Florida School Breakfast Program 2011). Time also emerges as a factor in deciding whether to eat lunch. Students in numerous focus groups have articulated their frustrations with time spent standing in the cafeteria line as well as lunch periods that are too short (Castillo and Lofton 2012; Orange County Public Schools 2014). The Orange County public school system reports that the average wait time in a lunch line is sixteen minutes for a high school student and twelve minutes for a middle school student (versus six minutes for elementary), leaving only ten minutes for a high school student and twelve minutes for a middle school student to eat their lunch (Orange County Public Schools 2014).

FRP school meals also apparently carry the stigma of "being on welfare," and that too is a barrier to participation. Public Law 108-265 (passed in 2004) prohibits the overt identification of students who are eligible for FRP, and measures such as universal free lunch, the CEP, and Provision 2 are also intended to remove this barrier. Still, Lisa Bailey-Davis and colleagues (2013) found that parents and children both perceive stigma attached to participation, and in this study students were sometimes ridiculed for selecting the free breakfast instead of purchasing items from the à la carte line. Similar concerns are reported by Gleason (1995), Donika Mirtcheva and Lisa Powell (2009), Elizabeth Potamites and Anne Gordon (2010), and Rajiv Bhatia, Paula Jones, and Zetta Reicker (2011). Mirtcheva and Powell (2009) found that high school students from low-income families are the age group most impacted by the stigma of the FRP lunch, with low-income minority students affected most of all.

Studies have also found that the food environment in the neighborhoods surrounding schools can impact participation in the school meal programs by providing alternatives viewed as preferable by students, particularly high school students who have increased autonomy and access to alternative methods of transportation apart from the school bus (Zenk and Powell 2008).

School Meals and Food Insecurity

Do the free and reduced-cost breakfast and lunch programs in the nation's public schools in fact improve the nutritional status of low-income students? There is no firm answer to the question. If all low-income students availed themselves of cafeteria breakfasts and lunches each day and ate everything on the plate, they would undoubtedly be better off nutritionally. But neither of these conditions prevails. In some school systems, upward of 80 percent of income-eligible students decline to participate and either skip meals or seek alternative food sources. Those who do eat in the school cafeterias routinely discard a quarter or more of the food they are served. Studies show that the items most likely to be discarded are the vegetable and fruit selections, precisely the food we would most want school children to eat. Depending on the specific item, manner of cooking and presentation, overall appearance, palatability, and like factors, a great deal of the protein, carbohydrates, and the like, is also discarded. Plate waste is now universally recognized as a limiting factor in the net nutrient value of school cafeteria meals. Still, many students eat in the cafeteria every day, sometimes twice a day, and eat most or all of what they are served. That none of this describes *all* students does not detract from and is not meant to belittle the very sizable nutritional benefits that many students receive from the school meal programs.

In 2014, under the leadership of Michelle Obama, the nutritional standards for free and reduced-cost school meals were enhanced, mainly to reduce fat, sodium, and total calories and increase the consumption of complex carbohydrates—all this to address the growing child obesity problem. Without doubt, childhood obesity is a serious problem, and with equal certainty, schoolchildren should be given healthy options in the school cafeteria. At the same time, it is better that children eat than not eat, and if many are choosing not to eat because they find the food unpalatable, perhaps the healthier option is to relax the nutritional standards.

The USDA says that kids will eventually get used to the new rules, come to accept them, and be healthier as a result, but the Government Accounting Office (2013) acknowledges that "modifications are needed to some of the new nutrition standards" because school food authorities have reported that the new standards have complicated meal planning, driven up the price of meals served, and generated even more plate waste than before. In one well-publicized protest in a rural Kentucky school district, schoolchildren were quoted as saying that "the food tastes like vomit," "the brown wheat bread is nasty," "the skim and one percent milk is gross," and "the nonfat strawberry- and chocolate-flavored drinks are disgusting" (see Chumley 2013). This does not make it sound as though kids will "get over" the new standards anytime soon. As an editorial in the *Topeka Capital-Journal* (2014) framed the issue, "What good are school lunches if kids won't eat them?"

SNAP

As of December 2015, there were 45.4 million persons enrolled in SNAP, representing 23.4 million households. This is about 15 percent of the total US population. The number of SNAP recipients nationwide has been above 40 million since 2010.[5] During the first decade of the new millennium, enrollment was right around 20–25 million. In short, SNAP participation has nearly doubled in the past several years, a surge most analysts attribute to the 2008–2009 recession and its lingering economic effects. As an item from the Center on Budget and Policy Priorities (Stone, Sherman, and Keith-Jennings 2015) put it, "No Mystery Why SNAP Enrollment Remains High: It's Still the Economy."

SNAP is by far the largest federal food-aid program in terms of both enrollment and expenditures. In 2011, expenditures for SNAP were about $84 billion (versus about $14 billion for the school breakfast and lunch programs and $7 billion for the Women, Infants, and Children program). And while SNAP spending is dwarfed by, say, the cost of Medicaid ($433 billion), SNAP expenditures in 2011 exceeded the total federal expenditure on all education programs combined ($60 billion). It clearly is reasonable to ask what the country gets back from its investment in SNAP.

History

The food stamp program was reauthorized as a permanent program by Congress in 1964 but was initially implemented in the 1930s as a way to dispose of agricultural surplus when so many were going hungry during the Great Depression. By the end of World War II, however, agricultural surpluses had ended along with the original food stamp program (Wilde 2013). At this point, many counties left the program, since they were no longer mandated to participate, leaving many of the nation's poorest counties unserved by any federal food assistance programs. It was not until the poverty investigations by a Senate subcommittee on employment and poverty and the subsequent CBS special "Hunger in America" in the 1960s that alarming levels of destitution, hunger, and even starvation were rediscovered and the food stamp program was resurrected as a potential solution (Poppendieck 1999). The official reauthorization of the food stamp program in 1964 allowed participants to purchase food stamps at a discounted rate in order to purchase federally mandated food. This continued until the Food Stamp Act of 1977, which transformed the program into an entitlement and eliminated the required purchase of food stamps. From 1977 forward, food stamp benefits have imposed no direct costs on participants.

Although the food stamp program was reenacted to combat the newly discovered problem of hunger in the United States, a second motivation was to put to good use surplus agricultural products that the federal government purchased as a price support measure for farmers. So while SNAP is a social program, it remains tied to the agricultural industry, is still housed under the USDA, and is reauthorized every five years (or so) as an item in the US Farm Bill. Today, SNAP is not the agricultural price support mechanism it once was, but SNAP dollars do make a major contribution to the national food economy via retail food purchases, and in this way the program continues to function as an agricultural subsidy. SNAP benefits account for about 10 percent of national food retail spending (Wilde 2013). About 85 percent of the retail business from SNAP goes to the large full-service supermarkets, with the remaining 15 percent distributed among small grocers, farmers' markets, specialty food retailers, and the like.[6]

According to Krissy Clark (2014), Walmart, one of the nation's largest grocery retailers, takes in about 18 percent of the total SNAP dollars annually, which is in the vicinity of $14 billion, or 4 percent of Walmart's total US sales. One study in Ohio also found that 15 percent of the Walmart work force participates in SNAP. Walmart's notoriously low wages are thus made possible in part by SNAP benefits.

Eligibility Requirements and Benefits

To be eligible for SNAP benefits in 2015, a household must have had a gross monthly income of less than 130 percent of the federal poverty line; had a net monthly income (after deductions that are applied to offset high housing burdens and child care expenses) less than 100 percent of the poverty line; and held less than $2,250 in assets.[7] Certain people are ineligible for SNAP regardless of their income: examples include people on strike, most college students, and undocumented immigrants. On the other side of the coin, persons already receiving TANF, Supplemental Security Income (SSI), and certain other assistance are automatically qualified ("categorically eligible") to receive SNAP benefits (Falk and Aussenberg 2014).

There are other criteria that must be met. SNAP recipients generally must be citizens. Able-bodied adults between ages eighteen and fifty must either have a job, be looking for work, or be actively participating in an employment training program. If the employment requirements are not met but the income and asset requirements are, benefits are limited to three months in every three-year period.

SNAP benefits vary widely. The average SNAP-participating household received $257.93 in monthly benefits in fiscal year 2015 while the average benefit for an individual was $126.90. To put these numbers in perspective, 100 percent of the federal poverty line for a single individual in 2015 was $11,770, with the benefit for twelve months being about $1,523. So the average SNAP benefit for an individual right at the poverty line would increase that individual's effective annual income by about 13 percent—far from trivial. At the same time, the closer a person rises to the poverty line, the lower the SNAP benefit, and vice versa. About half the poverty population earns half or less of the poverty income (or less than $6,000 per year), and for such persons the annual SNAP benefit would add about 25 percent to their purchasing power. Many low-income households depend critically on their monthly SNAP benefit.

In the wake of the Great Recession, SNAP participation increased drastically. In 2007, there were 26 million participants, and four years later, 45 million. Peak enrollment occurred in December 2012, when 47.8 million Americans received SNAP benefits. Since, enrollments have declined slightly, to 46.7 million in 2014 and about 42.6 million as of 2017.

SNAP is reauthorized periodically via the so-called Farm Bill and is controversial in every new iteration. The most recent reauthorization was in 2018. What was once a largely bipartisan effort to shore up the nation's farmers and agricultural interests has in recent decades become a bitter partisan battle between conservatives and liberals, the former intent on cutting and reworking SNAP, the latter committed to retaining the program in its current form. A Republican proposal for 2019 would have reduced the program budget by a third. In the process, the Farm Bill becomes an exercise in power versus an effort to address the food needs of the nation's low-income population. This is a classic illustration of the point that food insecurity in the United States has far more to do with politics than with the availability of food.

Participation Rates and Correlates

SNAP is an entitlement. This means that the federal government has committed to provide enough funds to the program to cover all eligible participants. Despite this guarantee, not all who are eligible participate (Delaney 2013). According to a 2011 USDA report on trends in SNAP participation, only 72 percent of eligible US households participate. If all eligible persons participated, the total SNAP population today would be in the vicinity 65 million people, nearly one American in five.

Working people who are SNAP-eligible (the "working poor") participate at particularly low rates. One study found that only 60 percent of the income-eligible working poor participated in 2009 (Leftin, Eslami, and Strayer 2011). Participation rates also vary sharply across states. California, Texas, and Florida have some of the lowest participation rates (below 70 percent of those eligible) while states like Washington, Oregon, Maine, and West Virginia have some of the highest (above 82 percent).

Participation in SNAP varies by a number of other factors. SNAP participation follows the prevailing poverty rates and overall economic climate but also responds to state and federal policy mandates (Mabli, Martin and Castner 2010; McKernan, Ratcliffe, and Rosenberg 2003; Andrews and Smallwood 2012; Tiehen, Jolliffe, and Gundersen 2012). At the household level, a USDA report (2016) shows that many SNAP households contain one or more dependent children (57 percent), at least one elderly person (16 percent), or someone who is disabled (20 percent). Thus, 93 percent of all SNAP households support either dependent children, elderly people, or disabled adults. The idea that huge numbers of SNAP recipients are able-bodied people who "could work if they wanted to" is simply wrong.

Sara Strickhouser (2016) used the 2013 Current Population Survey to confirm that the major predictors of SNAP participation are being female, being young, belonging to a minority group, being unmarried, being uneducated or disabled, and most of all being poor. Among income-qualified persons and households, the lowest rate of SNAP participation is found among those over age sixty. Only about a third of income-eligible seniors participate. Many factors contribute to this low participation rate, from barriers related to mobility, technology, and stigma to widespread myths about how the program works and who can qualify.

Some research shows that lack of awareness is less important to nonparticipation than the fact that the burden of the application and qualification process greatly outweighs the potential benefit (Clancy, Bowering, and Poppendieck 1989). Many food-insecure persons prefer either not to eat or to rely on emergency food assistance provided by food pantries and kitchens rather than deal with the hassles of SNAP (Poppendieck 1999).

The stigma of being on welfare is another major factor for all SNAP-eligible populations, especially seniors (McConnell, Ponza, and Cohen 1999; Geiger, Wilks, and Livermore 2014). One national survey of SNAP households showed that among households with seniors, 76 percent reported feelings of shame, embarrassment, or stigma compared to only 60 percent of all participating households.[8] In particular, seniors reported being worried about how they might be perceived by grocery store staff and other shoppers and about the embarrassment they might feel if family and friends knew they received SNAP benefits. Other studies (e.g., Levedahl, Ballenger, and Harold 1994; Dean 2008) reveal that the SNAP application process is often daunting. Many states now require that SNAP applications be completed and submitted online, a particular challenge for many seniors. Also, many of the questions on the application form seem unnecessary or cause seniors to feel guilty. For those with limited English proficiency, the forms seem especially confusing.

In short, in the minds of many, SNAP is "not for us" and they perceive it would be unfair to take resources away from those for whom they believe the program is intended, no matter how food-insecure they are. Looming above all other considerations, however, is that participation is mainly a function of the amount of benefits received. The USDA finds (indeed, has found for thirty-five consecutive years) that as benefits increase, so do participation rates, regardless of household type or demographic characteristics.

Demonization and Stigma

SNAP enrollments have fallen by more than 6 million since 2012 but remain nearly 70 percent higher today than they were when President

Barack Obama first took office. This has generated near hysteria in Republican circles. Obama was derided as "the food stamp president," conveniently ignoring that SNAP spending doubled under the George W. Bush administration before doubling again under Obama. Former Speaker of the House Newt Gingrich generated a national sound bite when he claimed that "more people have been put on food stamps by Barack Obama than any president in American history." In fact, Bush and Obama are about tied for this distinction. President Donald Trump proposed to cut more than $190 billion from the 2019 SNAP budget via stricter eligibility rules and additional work requirements and to replace EBT cards with boxes of food, evidently to make sure that the poor eat what we want them to eat. In the same vein, Missouri Republicans introduced a bill prohibiting SNAP recipients from using their SNAP benefits to buy steak, other cuts of beef, lobster, cookies, chips, energy drinks—even fish sticks and canned tuna. Kansas's guardians of the public trust passed a bill in 2015 that prohibited welfare recipients from withdrawing more than $25 in benefits per day and made it illegal to spend public aid on jewelry, tattoos, massages, spa treatments, lingerie, tobacco, movies, bail bonds, arcade games, and visits to swimming pools, fortunetellers, amusement parks, or ocean cruises.

Several other states have contemplated similar legislation. New Mexico Republicans introduced a bill that would require SNAP recipients to do community service, much like paroled felons. Other states, among them Virginia and Florida, have considered legislation requiring that all welfare recipients including SNAP participants be drug-tested, despite solid evidence that drug use and abuse are less common among SNAP recipients than the population at large. Rush Limbaugh was so incensed by the increase in SNAP enrollments that he proposed eliminating the SNAP program entirely. His advice to those truly in need: dumpster-diving.

A huge issue in conservative circles is that many SNAP participants are believed to be fraudulent—that is, they are alleged to be people with plenty of money who get themselves enrolled in the food stamp program so they can use their cash on beer, cigarettes, ocean cruises, tattoos, lottery tickets, and similar frivolities. According to the Center on Budget and Policy Priorities (2015), SNAP error rates have been *falling* for the past two decades and are now at an all-time low. Counting both overpayments and underpayments, the error rate is roughly 3.8 percent. At one time, states with error rates of less than

6 percent received enhanced funding in recognition of their "exemplary performance." In contrast, the Internal Revenue Service estimates that income-tax noncompliance is on the order of 17 percent of all returns. According to the Center on Budget and Policy Priorities, "SNAP has one of the most rigorous payment error measurement systems of any public benefit program" (Rosenbaum 2013:1). In 2013, something like a hundred million dollars' worth of SNAP benefits were redeemed at military commissaries and about a million US veterans were SNAP recipients.[9]

Why all the animosity directed against people on SNAP? The *Des Moines Register* (2015) has said all that needs to be said: "It's not because the poor are using more drugs or abusing public benefits. It's not to help them get jobs. It's not to save taxpayer money. It's because stereotyping this group of Americans is easier than actually helping them." In the end, people object to welfare because they cannot quite shake the thought that many welfare recipients are *unworthy,* that they are getting more than they *deserve.*

The USDA has taken some steps to reduce the stigma of SNAP participation and these need to be acknowledged. Until the 1990s, participants were required to purchase paper food stamps that were easily recognized in the supermarket line. Today, benefits are distributed through EBT cards that look like any other credit or debit card. The move to EBT cards was intended to reduce fraud and make the program more appealing to potential participants by reducing stigma.

One of the most serious problems posed by the political circus that surrounds the discussion of SNAP is that it diverts attention from some very real and serious issues with the program, issues that are widely discussed in the research literature but never make their way onto the public policy agenda. What if, for example, SNAP did little or nothing to improve the nutritional status of recipients, increased rather than decreased food insecurity, and was a probable cause of obesity among the poor? That any of these things is true is not known with certainty, but there is plenty of research to suggest that they may be.

SNAP and Nutrition

We begin on a technical point of methodology and the issue of "selection effects." The general problem is as follows. Even in a population of income-eligible persons and households, some people will choose to participate in SNAP and others will not. Clearly, each group does so for its own reasons, so the two groups will differ in ways other than their SNAP participation. If those other ways in which they differ are related to an outcome of interest (say, obesity or food insecurity), then straight comparisons between the two groups can be dangerously misleading.

A hypothetical example illustrates the problem. Not all low-income persons are food-insecure; some manage their food supply quite adequately without SNAP assistance. Those who are already food-secure would be less motivated to enroll in SNAP. In contrast, other low-income persons are highly food-insecure so their motivation to enroll would be strong. If we then compare the food-insecurity scores of people who enrolled in SNAP with those who did not, we would see that SNAP enrollees were more food-insecure and might conclude, erroneously, that SNAP caused food insecurity to increase, when in fact it was food insecurity that caused SNAP participation to increase. Marianne Bitler (2014) points out that correlational studies that do not control for such "entering differences" can therefore mislead. For this reason, the only truly credible studies are multivariate analyses that control statistically for selection differences.

A case in point is the effect of SNAP participation on nutritional adequacy, a topic that has been researched extensively. The Center for Budget and Policy Priorities (2015) states that "SNAP enables low-income households to afford more healthy foods." But this does not mean that SNAP participants purchase healthier foods, only that they *might*. They also might purchase more of the same unhealthy food they have been buying for years. The causal argument here assumes that economics are a larger barrier to healthy eating than culture, custom, or tradition. But is this true empirically?

Angela Hilmers and colleagues (2014) measured the association between SNAP participation and diet quality among 661 Hispanic women aged twenty-six to forty-four living in Texas. Across the sample, most women did not meet established dietary guidelines, and SNAP participants reported less healthy diets than eligible nonparticipants. Similarly, using four waves of NHANES data from 2003 to 2010, Binh Nyguen and colleagues (2015) concluded that SNAP participants had lower overall dietary quality as compared to income-eligible nonparticipants.

The best review of available research on the issue of nutritional adequacy and SNAP is by Tatiana Andreyeva, Amanda Tripp, and Marlene Schwartz (2015), who reviewed twenty-five published studies. All twenty-five studies were peer-reviewed, published between 2003 and 2014, used high quality US data, and provided data on dietary quality and intake of SNAP participants and nonparticipants (i.e., outcomes other than food insecurity or obesity). All but three studies used extensive multivariate analyses to control—at least partially—for selection effects. Three studies attempted to demonstrate causality using complex instrumental variables and maximum-likelihood approaches, and these three studies were given the greatest weight.

Across the twenty-five studies, "daily caloric, macronutrient, and micronutrient intake of SNAP participants did not differ systematically from those of income-eligible nonparticipants" (p. 594). "Did not differ" means that SNAP participation neither increased nor decreased dietary intake. "However, differences in dietary quality emerged. Adult SNAP participants scored *lower* on the Healthy Eating Index than either group of nonparticipants. Children's diets were similar among SNAP participants and low-income nonparticipants, but were less nutritious than diets of higher-income children" (p. 594, emphasis added). A review by the USDA (2016) likewise found little or no difference between SNAP participants and nonparticipants on dietary intake.

Exceptions to the "no differences" findings were noted for certain subgroups. For example, one study found that SNAP-participating younger women consumed more calories than non-SNAP women of the same age, but this effect was not consistently demonstrated across studies. Most studies found no significant differences in fresh fruit and vegetable consumption between enrollees and non-enrollees. There is some evidence that SNAP increases whole fruit consumption and consumption of certain other nutrients, but the differences are not large and not consistent across studies. Results on a Healthy Eating Index showed that no group met dietary recommendations whether they were enrolled in SNAP or not. (For additional confirmation of the "no differences" findings, see also Leung et al. 2014; Hilmers et al. 2014.)

What do we make of the general pattern of results? One certain conclusion is that if SNAP does in fact promote healthier eating, the effect is too small to make itself known in large national surveys. A more aggressive conclusion would be that SNAP has no effect on the nutritional sufficiency of diets consumed by the low-income population. Being on SNAP does not result in more calories being consumed or any other nutrient advantage.

For years it has been assumed that SNAP participants do not eat a healthier diet than nonparticipants because low-income people in general do not understand what a truly healthy diet looks like. This hypothesis has some merit, as discussed earlier. One study of SNAP-eligible persons found that only 44 percent had adequate health literacy (Song, Grutzmacher, and Kostenko 2014). The same study found large gaps between health self-perception and objective health status and between perceived and actual obesity. In response to concerns about nutritional knowledge, as part of the Healthy, Hunger-Free Kids Act of 2010, Congress authorized about $400 million to fund SNAP-Ed, which provides grants to the states to develop and implement nutrition education and obesity prevention programs.

Does SNAP Improve Health?

Since SNAP seems to have limited or no effect on what or how much people eat, one would not expect SNAP participation to have much of an effect on health. And indeed, the large literature that exists on this topic is a morass of inconsistent and contradictory findings. SNAP participation does seem to increase subjective health status. Using nationally representative survey data and an "unobserved variables" multivariate modeling analysis, Christian Gregory and Partha Deb (2015) found that SNAP participation was consistently and positively related to subjective health status. The data also showed that SNAP participants had fewer days in bed due to illness, fewer doctor visits, and fewer outpatient visits. Not all studies report the same findings, but many do.

If SNAP has no apparent effect on diet, how would SNAP participation affect perceived health? Gregory and Deb note that "it is reasonable to assume that, because SNAP reduces food insecurity and gives households extra income, it might also have an ameliorative effect on conditions associated with food hardship and improve health in general." In other words, SNAP may free up household resources for "activities that promote well-being but are not necessarily diet-related" (p. 11).

To be food-secure, according to the official USDA definition, one must have sufficient access to *nutritious* food. While SNAP benefits may increase caloric intake, recipients are free to purchase whatever foods they like, and those often include processed or less healthy foods (Andreyeva, Tripp, and Schwartz 2015). In general,

SNAP users do spend more on less nutritious, processed foods than on wholesome foods like milk, meat, and fruits and vegetables (Pringle 2013) and consume less than the recommended amount of whole grains, fruits, vegetables, fish, and nuts (Leung et al. 2012).

Does SNAP Participation Cause Obesity?

Because of these concerns over health outcomes and how they are affected by SNAP, research has attempted to link SNAP use to a number of different chronic diseases. These include diabetes, overweight, and obesity. SNAP usage and its connection to obesity remains the most controversial issue. Some feel SNAP benefits encourage the purchase of sugary, high-calorie, cheap foods and that poor food purchase choices may be leading to increased obesity among SNAP users (Shenkin and Jacobson 2010). However, the evidence is inconsistent—sometimes it appears that SNAP increases obesity and sometimes it does not (Dinour, Bergen, and Yeh 2007; Franklin et al. 2012). The most consistent finding is a link between SNAP participation and obesity among women (Townsend et al. 2001; Franklin et al. 2012). Whether this is also true for adult men and children of either gender remains undetermined (Holben 2010). The most recent study, a May 2015 study by the USDA, confirms the connection between obesity and SNAP participation (Condon et al. 2015), but this comes at the end of a long line of studies that are characterized by inconsistent results.

Why might SNAP increase obesity? One hypothesis is that the availability of SNAP resources "enables" the purchase of more fattening and unhealthy food. Children in SNAP households consume more sugary beverages than children in non-SNAP households. But subtler effects may also be involved—for example, the proposed "food acquisition cycle" proposed by Parke Wilde and Christine Ranney (2000).

Conclusion

None of the public policy initiatives we have discussed solves the food-insecurity problem in its target population, and none is intended to do so. Meals on Wheels is intended to help frail seniors age in place. School breakfast and lunch programs are intended to augment food received in the home. And the "S" in SNAP stands for "supplemental." We have no public policy in place whose intention is specifically to eliminate food insecurity in the American population. Perhaps we should.

Yet it is obvious that almost all persons and families in the United States manage to feed themselves more or less adequately; otherwise we would have body wagons in the streets every morning removing the corpses of those who starved to death the previous evening. (The number of Americans who starve to death annually is on the order of a few thousand at most.) Through some combination of personal resources, private acts of charity, scavenging, self-provisioning, and public policy programs, most people manage to get enough calories into their stomachs most of the time. The serious policy question is just how much of a struggle we want the daily quest for adequate nutrition to be. Is an all-out multipronged effort to reduce food insecurity in the United States too much to ask? Are these not the dues we must pay to claim membership in the community of civilized nations?

Notes

1. Michael Ponza, James Ohls, and Barbara Millen (1996) surveyed a national sample of Meals on Wheels participants. Nearly 90 percent reported receiving only one meal (lunch) daily.

2. Feeding programs for qualifying seniors located in facilities that house seniors or in senior centers, church basements, and the like. Congregate feeding is for ambulatory seniors; meals are delivered to the site and people are fed in a group setting; home-delivered meals are (generally) for seniors with ambulation challenges. Most of the research we review in this chapter is focused on the home-delivered-meals program. Useful exceptions more focused on the congregate programs are Lee and Gould 2012 and Thomas, Ghiselli, and Almanza 2011.

3. The specific activities of daily living in question are personal grooming, eating, getting in and out of bed, walking, taking a bath or shower, using the toilet, dressing, and getting to the bathroom on time.

4. This section is coauthored with J. Dillon Caldwell, Mandi Barringer, and Brenda Savage.

5. See http://www.fns.usda.gov/pd/supplemental-nutrition-assistance -program-snap.

6. See http://yourbusiness.azcentral.com/effects-food-stamps-grocery -industry-11777.html.

7. This is the limit for households with no elderly or disabled member. If there is an elderly or disabled member of the household, the asset limit is $3,250 (as of 2015). At one time, the asset test was waived for such households, but no more.

8. See "Stigma Plays a Particularly Important Role" at http://mediamatters .org/research/2012/06/29/right-wing-media-attacks-snap-outreach-to-elder /185663.

9. See https://www.nfesh.org/food-stamps-military-families-redeem-100 -million-a-year-in-snap-benefits.

7

Feeding the World in
the Twenty-First Century

We have argued throughout this book that food insecurity is a problem of access and distribution more than a supply problem, but not everyone agrees with this conclusion. The United Nations (2009) has declared that global food production "must double by 2050." The idea that we will need twice as much food in 2050 as we require today to keep up with global population growth has been advanced hundreds of times by scores of scholars, activists, nonprofit leaders, and government officials, often with dire predictions (malnutrition, starvation, mass death) if we fail. Barriers include insufficient global investment in agriculture, failures in local production and delivery infrastructure, declining food safety nets, gross overconsumption in the more affluent nations, the inefficiencies of meat-based diets, and climate change. So we conclude the book with some thoughts on the world food supply.

The current world population stands at 7 billion people. According to the US Census Bureau, that specific figure was reached on March 12, 2011, and has since increased to about 7.6 billion (Worldometers n.d.). Demographic projections out to 2050 put the world population thirty-five years from now at somewhere between 8.3 and 10.9 billion. If we split the difference, then by 2050 the world population will be somewhere around 9.6 billion, or roughly a 37 percent total increase. That is certainly a significant increase but nowhere close to a doubling. So if the population will increase by 37 percent, why does food production need to double?

The assumption is that as the world population continues to increase, so will global affluence, and with increasing affluence, especially in the emerging nations (or more generally the global South), will come changing dietary preferences and behavior that will amplify the world need for food. Specifically, the newly affluent are expected to increase their consumption of meat, dairy, and total calories and decrease their consumption of roots, tubers, and vegetables. In this manner, an approximately 40 percent increase in population becomes a 100 percent increase in the demand for food.

Demographic predictions are notoriously unreliable—highly sensitive to their entering assumptions. Predictions about cultural change are even more so. Certainly, we can say that the world demand for food will increase in the next three or four decades, probably by a substantial amount. Saying much more than that is to engage in hyperbole. (Interestingly, after 2050, the rate of growth is projected to level off and then begin to decline, so the expectation is that the food crisis will abate after 2050.)

In addition to increased agricultural production, we will also need to develop agricultural practices that are sustainable over the long term. Present practices are generally assumed not to be sustainable. A United Nations Environment Programme (UNEP) report prepared by Edgar Hertwich and colleagues (2010) concluded that fossil fuel use and agricultural production are major environmental stressors. The overall environmental impacts of agricultural production were found to be greater than most other forms of production (for example the production of cement and other manufactured goods). Agriculture is energy- and water-intensive (both increasingly scarce commodities), generates problematic waste streams (chicken manure, for example), and adds to habitat loss, soil depletion, biodiversity loss, and climate change. These impacts are expected to increase sharply as population grows and as global affluence increases, as a doubling of income apparently leads to an 80 percent increase in an individual's environmental impact.

In the end, the world consumption of meat is said to lie at the heart of the problem; eating more meat is the principal means by which extra income translates into environmental impact. That the world at large cannot consume an average American diet is an article of faith in many food advocacy circles. The only sustainable way to feed the world in the near-term future is a substantial worldwide diet change toward vegetables and away from meat. The UNEP report is one of scores or even hundreds of recent analyses that indict the Western diet, especially the US diet, as environmentally unsustainable.

The simultaneous need for more production and more sustainability in the methods of production has been called the "oxymoron of sustainable intensification" (Tomlinson 2011:82). "Sustainable intensification" is the hopeful thought that science will find some way to significantly increase (intensify) world food production but without any further environmental degradation or greater consumption of natural resources. Many commentators see this as a self-evidently silly proposition and conclude that the only alternative to Malthusian catastrophe is a radical change in the dietary habits of the global North to a plant-based diet.

The case in point on both sides of this discussion is the so-called Green Revolution, the dramatic changes in world agricultural production that occurred in the second half of the twentieth century. The Green Revolution was based on newly available chemical fertilizers and synthetic herbicides and pesticides along with the development of high-yield, disease-resistant strains of many crops—wheat initially, with other crops (rice, corn, etc.) quick to follow. Rapid worldwide adoption of Green Revolution practices produced a sharp increase in yields per acre that is generally credited with saving a billion or so people from starvation (and making farming a far more lucrative business than ever before). The Green Revolution was transformative in places such as Mexico, Brazil, India, the Philippines, and Africa. So what's to say that an even Greener Revolution is not in the offing, that even today science stands on the edge of technological advances that will readily meet mid-twenty-first-century food demand?

Critics respond by pointing to the downside of the Green Revolution. Sure, hundreds of millions—maybe billions—of people were spared, but at what cost? Among the costs often mentioned in these discussions are that croplands once devoted to subsistence agriculture were shifted into production of grains for export or to be used for animal feed (for example, wheat substituted for beans, as in the Indian case), with a resulting *increase* in food insecurity. Also, by switching from traditional to high-yield seed stock, biodiversity declined. Reliance on artificial fertilizers and pest control products and carbon fuels rather than human labor increased greenhouse gas emissions and fostered climate change. Mass agricultural production drove out many small producers (peasants) and thus fueled rural-to-urban migration (with all the problems that this has caused). The Green Revolution has led to worldwide dependence on nonrenewable resources to feed the population, widespread adoption of artificial pesticides has created health problems in developing nations, and mechanization of agriculture has caused many farmers to go deeply into debt, caused unemployment in agricultural regions, increased income inequalities, and exacerbated class divisions in traditional societies.

Although this list is by no means complete, it forms the general basis for the oft-stated conclusion that the Green Revolution is unsustainable. The carrying capacity of the planet and its environment is finite; resources like energy, water, and fertile soil are limited; the globe is overpopulated; and all this will only get worse unless there are fewer people or radical changes in the human diet, meaning specifically less meat and dairy and fewer calories overall.

One has to wonder, though, whether global poverty is sustainable but affluence is not. Is our only choice between failing to feed the planet's population and giving up chicken, pork, and beef? Is the American fondness for hamburgers the end-source of insufficient millet in the food baskets of Egyptian peasants? Is there no reason to hope that sustainable efficiencies of production can increase the global supply of food without wreaking havoc on the environment? Is pessimism about the future inevitable?

Many of these questions are effectively unanswerable given the current state of knowledge, but there is plenty of research to suggest that the future need not be as bleak or unsatisfactory as the doomsday scenarios suggest. Of necessity, these worrisome scenarios are all based on projections into an indefinite future, and historically, realities often manage to thwart the most elegant projections.

"Doubling Production" as an Ideological Frame

"Within the emergent international policy arena of 'food insecurity,' the imperative to double global food production by 2050 has become ubiquitous" (Tomlinson 2011:81). Among government ministers and bureaucrats, engaged academics, and food policy advocates, this has become "an accepted figure that everybody repeats," a "dominant framing" of the food-security problem. (For a well-known and tightly reasoned exposition of the "doubling" frame, see Godfray et al. 2010.) The issue is whether this framing is the inevitable consequence of the best available science or, as Isobel Tomlinson puts it, "a key discursive device being used by institutions and individuals with prior ideological commitment to a particular framing of the food security issue" (2011:81).

To begin, although the "doubling" claims are presented as "what we need to do" to avoid Malthusian catastrophe, the original source for the claim (a United Nations Food and Agriculture Organization report [2009] based on fancy econometric modeling) explicitly denies any normative aspirations. The report is intended to reflect a "most likely" future, not a "most desirable" one and even less an "inevitable" one. In the reinterpretation of the report's intent, proponents have embraced that "oxymoron of sustainable intensification," the "truism" that the "most likely scenario is that more food will need to be produced from the same or less land" (p. 2). A second implication is that the only (or best) way to do this is to grow food to feed people directly, not to grow food to feed animals that then feed people. Hence, the insistence on a shift to plant-based diets becomes an essential element in the framing.

The "doubling" frame assumes that as economies grow in developing countries, their citizens will eat less carbohydrate-rich staples (grains, roots, tubers) and more meat, dairy, and sugar, with devastating effects not only on the world supply of food but also on personal health. "Indeed, the enormity of the global food security challenge has been discursively constructed on the basis that the imperative to meet the projections of increasing demand, based on the dietary choices of an increasing, wealthier, population in the Global South is taken as a given. . . . [J]ust feeding a growing population wouldn't be too bad a task . . . but it becomes a much larger task with the increase in per capita income and a shift toward a more Western diet. In fact the scale of the increased demand is based not solely on increases in the Global South, but also on the maintenance (and small increase) of very high levels of consumption (of calories and meat and dairy) in the Global North" (Tomlinson 2011:4). The implication, often quite explicit, is ironic: the global North must learn to eat more like the global South so that the global South can eat more like the global North.

A key premise in the "doubling" perspective is that diets are driven mostly by economics and that, as the world becomes more affluent, there will be increased demand for Western-style diets. But as we have stressed throughout this volume, dietary preferences are also determined by religious beliefs, custom and habit, cultural forces, and many other non-economic factors. The assumption that diets become increasingly unsustainable as affluence increases is not a confirmed scientific fact known to hold around the world but rather an assumption based on differences in consumption by incomes in the United States and a few other places. What newly affluent factory workers in Brazil or Mali will choose to eat and how that compares with what they eat now is undetermined.

The "doubling" frame sees food insecurity solely as a problem of insufficient agriculture production and thus ignores the problems of access, utilization, and distribution. Adopting Amartya Sen's perspective (1981), we might say that a 70 percent or even 100 percent increase in food production will not in itself increase the global entitlement to food if issues of access and distribution remain unresolved. Even the United Nations Food and Agriculture Organization report (2009) concedes that "access to food [by those in poverty] will require a proper socio-economic framework to address imbalances and inequalities." The "doubling" frame excludes such considerations from the policy discussion around global food insecurity.

Tomlinson concludes that the "doubling" frame results as much from theoretical ideological commitments as from available scientific findings. But what is the ideological or strategic advantage that ensues? First, the frame contains an implicit critique of the inadequacies of world food production and distribution systems and is therefore congenial toward those who see Western capitalism as the ultimate root of evil in the world. Within the frame, too, are many reasons to encourage a shift toward vegetarian diets, a goal that many favor for reasons ranging from personal health to animal rights. The frame embraces a commitment to a liberalization of global agricultural trade that would "spread risks, encourage growth, keep prices competitive, increase the diversity of supply, and incentivize production" (Tomlinson 2011:5)—all highly desirable to nations that consume a great deal more than their fair share of the global food supply. Finally, in describing the problem as mainly one of production, the far thornier and more difficult issues of access and distribution are avoided.

The Oxymoron Resolved: Can Scientific Developments Increase Both Production and Sustainability?

Let us assume that global food production needs to increase substantially between now and 2050 and that at the same time the sustainability of food production must also increase. Greater sustainability would seemingly require a return to earlier agricultural practices: using manure, for example, rather than artificial fertilizers; more serious crop rotation; using traditional rather than artificial methods of pest control; the end to monocultural farming practices; and large reductions in or complete abandonment of the consumption of meat and dairy. Abandoning the efficiencies and yields associated with Green Revolution farming practices would, however, tend to thwart the goal of increasing the food supply. Reconciling the "oxymoron" would therefore seemingly require a massive increase in acreage under production. But acreage under production has been declining, not increasing, as more and more land in the less developed societies is being grabbed by developers, foreign investors, and governments themselves to be pressed into nonagricultural use (or shifted away from growing food for local consumption and toward high-profit crops grown for exportation—sugar cane, palm oil, soybeans).

So what is the world to do? At the risk of being dismissed as modern-day Pollyannas, we cautiously suggest a more upbeat view of what modern science might accomplish. Successfully feeding the world's population, while daunting, is perhaps no more daunting than landing humans on the moon or decoding the human genome or inventing and institutionalizing the World Wide Web. Rather than simply assuming the impossibility of the task, let us instead review a dozen or so current scientific developments that might eventually resolve the oxymoron of sustainable intensification.

Water

Water is essential for agriculture and is one of the natural resources demanded by modern agricultural practices. The agricultural demand for freshwater is enormous. About 5 gallons of freshwater are required to grow a single almond; 240 gallons are required to grow the wheat in a single loaf of bread; 1,800 gallons of water are necessary to produce a single pound of beef; and so on. In the United

States, agriculture is responsible for about 80 percent of all water consumption. The recent California drought and its effects on national food production and prices serve to remind us just how dependent we are on a cheap and effectively limitless water supply.

There is, of course, no real shortage of water. Seventy percent of the planet is covered in the stuff and the natural cycle of evaporation and rain make water a renewable resource. But in many parts of the country and the world, fresh water suitable for drinking and agriculture is in short supply. Even now in the United States there have been local political controversies over which states and municipalities have the right to draw water from the Great Lakes. In other regions, groundwater is also being drawn more rapidly than the aquifers can be recharged by rain, with consequent restrictions on growth and development in the affected regions.

Some foods have a much larger "water footprint" than others, so one response to the water shortage has been to alter diets. The chief villain: beef. Cattle drink water, graze on grass that can grow only with water, eat grains that also require lots of water, and use lots of water in being transformed into roasts, steaks, and hamburger. While growing beef consumes the most water per pound of yield, other meats (pork, chicken, and the grains to feed them) are only marginally better. And the water consumed in manufacturing highly processed foods such as candy, snack foods, and ready-to-eat meals also gives these food products heavy water footprints. From a water-wasting viewpoint, dairy products are also hopeless: 382 gallons of water are required to produce a pound of cheese; 284 gallons to produce one gallon of milk. The inevitable conclusion is that eliminating animal-based foods from the diet can significantly aid in water conservation efforts. Eat less beef, milk, and cheese and more cabbage, strawberries, onions, lettuce, carrots, eggplant, grapefruit, and tomatoes (these foods have the slimmest water footprints). For protein, you'll need to rely mainly on tofu and other soy- and bean-based meat substitutes.

An alternative to reducing big-water-footprint foods in the diet is to increase the availability of freshwater suitable for agricultural use. This means either finding and exploiting new water resources or making more efficient use of the resources currently available. The purest water is harvested from underground aquifers, so this is the preferred source for drinking water. But much groundwater is also consumed in watering grass and for agriculture; in places like

Florida, half of household water consumption is used up in lawn maintenance. Surface water (waters from lakes and ponds) is not generally suitable for direct human consumption without a great deal of chemical processing but is certainly suitable for watering lawns, crops, and pasture; many farms in the US Midwest are irrigated today with surface water. Then too, a great deal of groundwater is consumed in showering, bathing, laundry, and like activities and nearly all of it just goes down the drain when it could be captured and reused, for example, in watering grass. The recent experience in many California cities is that home water consumption can be reduced by nearly half simply with more conservation and better use of the water that is now wasted. It is easy to imagine homes with one water supply hooked up to sinks and faucets; another connected to washing machines and toilets; and still a third harvesting household gray water, rain water, water pumped from home swimming pools, and the like, to be used strictly for lawn and garden irrigation. Many municipalities already offer reclaimed-water services to residents.

It is also clear that crop-water productivity (the yield of agricultural product per unit of water consumed) is suboptimal in many places and could be improved almost everywhere. Kate Brauman, Stefan Siebert, and Jonathan Foley note that "irrigation consumes more water than any other human activity, and thus the challenges of water sustainability and food security are closely linked" (2013:1). They also document "considerable variability" in crop-water productivity both across and within different climatic zones. Thus, in many agrarian regions, "farmers have substantial opportunities to improve water productivity"—that is, to get more food out of the ground for every gallon of water put in. "Water productivity could be increased by increasing yields via improved soil nutrient conditions and reduced wind-driven erosion. Examples of other interventions that have demonstrated improvements in water productivity include: rainwater harvesting and local water storage, applying drip or deficit irrigation, adjusting planting dates, and modifying tillage practices to reduce evaporation. In many cases, techniques for increasing water productivity, especially when it is low, require little or no additional water" (p. 6). And what difference would it make? If crop-water productivity in the most precipitation-limited regions were raised to the twentieth percentile of productivity (chosen because "this is a plausible level of increase"), that alone would provide sufficient food for about 110 million extra people.

In the longer run, desalination of water harvested from the oceans promises a virtually inexhaustible water supply. Places like Aruba have gotten by on desalinated water for decades, and while currently available technologies produce pure drinking water at unacceptably high costs per gallon, a recent report in the *MIT Technology Review* (Talbot 2015) hints at great progress in bringing down the per-gallon cost of desalinated water in the near-term future. The case is based largely on the development of the Sorek water desalination plant in Tel Aviv, Israel, which "produces clean water from the sea cheaply and at a scale never before achieved." This plant and three others now produce about 40 percent of Israel's water supply. Based on many engineering innovations, including some fundamental breakthroughs in reverse osmosis technology, the Sorek plant consumes far less energy than conventional desalination methods and makes a profit selling pure water for 58 cents per 1,000 liters, higher than but competitive with the cost of water from conventional sources.

Genetically Modified Organisms

Genetically modified organisms (GMOs) are organisms or strains of organisms that have been created through gene-splicing techniques or genetic engineering. All the traits of any living organism, plant or animal, are determined by the organism's genes: the color of a person's hair, the number of kernels on an ear of corn, the skeleton of a bird, *everything*. It is therefore possible in theory, and increasingly in fact, to modify genes to abolish undesirable traits and enhance desirable ones. When applied to agriculture, this would mean, for example, that strains of grains are disease-resistant, drought-tolerant, and intrinsically high-yield. No one disputes that GMOs can make plants and animals more disease-resistant, keep produce ripe longer, widen the range of conditions under which plants and animals can grow, promote more robust growth, reduce costs, increase yields, and provide economic benefits to farmers. There is little doubt that if we allowed it, GMOs could readily "feed the world" sustainably and more or less indefinitely. The barriers are not technological but rather political.

In the popular mind, genetically modified organisms seem to mean bacterial Frankensteins, cows with dozens of teats, three-headed sheep, six-foot-long carrots, and a whole bunch of rogue microorganisms against which the human body has no defense. Opponents are fond of mentioning that GMOs are banned outright in about thirty nations around the world, including Australia, Japan, and the entire European Union, because (or so it is alleged) GMOs are not considered to have been proven safe. But people in the United States have been consuming GMO foods for more than a decade with no apparent ill effects. "Much of the corn, soybean, sugar beets and cotton cultivated in the United States today contains plants whose DNA was manipulated in labs to resist disease and drought, ward off insects and boost the food supply" (Olster 2013). One wonders how much of the European resistance to GMOs is motivated by a concern for food safety and how much is just another form of protectionism that promotes domestic products over imported ones. (See Olster 2013 for a review of the key points in the GMO debate.)

People have been eating genetically modified organisms for 10,000 years, since the advent of agriculture. Selective breeding and cross-breeding have been common agricultural methods ever since some ancient agrarian decided to retain the seeds of the most productive plants as the basis of next year's crop, or to cross-breed the fastest-growing male sheep with the tastiest females. All this was assuredly "genetic engineering," but by natural methods rather than laboratory ones.

There is legitimate debate about the proper safety testing of GMO products before they are allowed on the market, about the open labeling of GMO foods, and about the proper role of these products in the global agricultural market. It is also clear that to this point, the main beneficiaries of GMOs have not been hungry peasants in the developing world but rather giant agribusinesses who have used genetic modification to increase profits as much as to feed a hungry world. The vast majority of GMO innovation has gone into increasing yields of large cash crops (corn, cotton, soy beans, wheat), not crops that feed the most people in the developing world (cassava, sorghum, millet). But none of these legitimate points belies the fact that genetic engineering is a powerful mechanism for increasing food production, a mechanism that can be applied to millet or pulses no less than to wheat or cotton or corn.

GMOs are already in the marketplace, and while they have not yet been proven conclusively to be safe, neither have they been proven not to be. The experience in the United States suggests that they are safe for widespread cultivation. Drought-, blight-, insect-, and disease-resistant plant and animal cultivars could immediately increase global food production by a factor of two or more in a few years. More exotic applications—for example, using genetic engineering to "super-charge" photosynthesis (Bullis 2015), which is now known to be feasible, or exploiting so-called CRISPR techniques to accelerate gene manipulation—promise even greater productivity gains within the decade. In the end, there is little doubt that GMOs could in principle "feed the world" more than adequately in the coming decades.

The strongest counterargument, that GMOs cannot feed the world, is based on the observation that these tools have been around for decades and have done more to increase agribusiness corporate profits than to feed the poor and hungry. Undoubtedly this is true. But it is a contingent truth, not a necessary truth. It describes the world as it has been, not as it needs to be.

Phosphorous, nitrogen, and potassium are essential plant nutrients and the components of most artificial fertilizers. Phosphate rock, which is currently the main source of phosphorus, is a nonrenewable resource. The high-quality reserves of phosphate rock are becoming increasingly scarce. Dan Cordell and Stuart White (2014) project peak phosphorus production to occur before 2035, after which demand will exceed supply. In other words, phosphorous scarcity will be a limiting condition on food availability well before the world population peaks around 2050. A further complication is that just five countries control about 90 percent of world phosphorous production: Morocco, China, South Africa, the United States, and Jordan.

Phosphorous scarcity in the coming decades will require more efficient agricultural use of phosphorous. Much of the Green Revolution has resulted from widespread, indiscriminate use of phosphorous- and nitrogen-based fertilizers mainly because the constituent elements are cheap, widely available, and effective. One result has been eutrophication of watersheds and their component lakes, rivers, bayous, and lagoons—an immense environmental problem in wetlands. And there has been a consequent movement to reduce fertilizer use, both in agriculture and in home lawn maintenance.

Abatement of eutrophication alone will increase efficiencies in the use of phosphorous fertilizers. There is also an effort to reduce, recover, and reuse phosphates. With respect to "reduce," it is now known with certainty that phosphorous- and nitrogen-based fertilizers are grossly overapplied. The amount of phosphorous required to maintain a healthy crop is extremely variable; it depends on what the crop is, local soil conditions, geography, weather, and other factors. It is therefore difficult for farmers, particularly small producers, to know the "just right" amount to spread on their fields. On the theory that if some is good, more is better, the net result is therefore overuse. Overuse is being addressed through simple technologies such as the Wisconsin SnapPlus software application that allows farmers to calculate an optimal fertilization plan from a few key inputs.

Recovery and reuse of phosphate resources are also growing rapidly. Once consumed, the principal method by which phosphorous goes back into the environment is via animal waste (manure). Excessive manure is a serious problem in the production of both pork and poultry; efficient recovery of waste phosphorous would turn manure from a nuisance to a valuable byproduct of production. Technologies to recover phosphorous from urine and manure are already well-developed and the object of intense worldwide research. As early as 2007, 53 percent of sewer sludge in the European Union was being reused in agriculture, a percentage that is certain to increase as phosphorous supplies decline.

Much the same can be said for nitrogen, a second major component of modern fertilizers (Spiertz 2010). Waste nitrogen is not as easily concentrated as waste phosphorous, so the nitrogen emphasis is more on efficient use than on recovery, and the goal is to increase yield with less nitrogen. As with phosphorous, this requires determining optimal nitrogen levels given local conditions and avoiding nitrogen overuse, but the technologies to do this are rapidly developing.

Multiple-cropping systems that rotate crops or involve multiple crops growing simultaneously can also increase nitrogen-use efficiency. It has been recognized for centuries that some crops (such as legumes, clover, soy beans, peanuts) affix atmospheric nitrogen to root nodules that then release nitrogen into the soil when the plant dies. Crop rotations that include these nitrogen-fixing plants naturally increase the fertility of the soil and are widely used in traditional and organic farming. This is less true of industrial agriculture only because commercially available nitrogen and phosphorous fertilizers are cheap; as they become more expensive, the economic attractiveness of crop-rotation practices increases.

* * *

There is no end to the list of recent and pending scientific advances that might greatly improve crop yields without an equivalent degree of environmental damage or resource depletion. Swati Chakraborty and Adrian Newton (2011), for example, discuss new strategies for pest and disease management under conditions of climate change. Climate change, they conclude, will exacerbate these problems but a variety of tools exist to manage them effectively, with genetic engineering at the head of the list. "Transgenic solutions must receive serious consideration in integrated disease management strategies to improve food security" (p. 11). Likewise, Mamadou Diallo and Jeffrey Brinker (2011) review an entire range of nanotechnologies that could potentially address issues of environment, water, food, mineral, and climate conditions as these might affect agricultural production. For example, in the past decade, significant progress has been made in developing nanotechnologies that "provide efficient, cost-effective, and environmentally sustainable solutions for supplying potable water for human use and clean water for agricultural and industrial uses" (p. 227); these technologies address water treatment, desalination, and water reuse. "Advances in nanotechnology could [also] result in major improvements in the technologies used to grow, process, store, and distribute food" (p. 228); these advances are in areas such as use of nanotechnology to diagnose and treat plant diseases, new food-packaging systems, detection of food-borne toxins and bacteria, and on through a long list.

Xin-Ping Chen et al. (2011) describe an experiment in China using an integrated soil-crop management system to grow maize. They used a hybrid-maize simulation model to "identify the most appropriate combination of planting date, crop density, and plant variety to use at a given site" (p. 6400). Average yields were about twice the yield achieved by current farming practices, with no increase in nitrogen fertilizer use. Riccardo Bommarco, David Kleijn, and Simon Potts (2013) summarize what is known about "ecological intensification" to enhance agricultural productivity—that is, to use natural ecosystems in the management of agricultural practice. These strategies are presented as an alternative approach to achieving Green Revolution yields but with fewer and less destructive environmental impacts. But these strategies can also be seen as complementary to Green Revolution practices—especially in areas such as soil formation and nutrient cycling, biological pest control, crop pollination, and biodiversity conservation.

The preceding paragraphs have summarized just a few of the many scores of research papers published in the past few years that give a basis for optimism that the "oxymoron of sustainable intensification" is perhaps not so moronic after all. Not all the innovations and solutions hinted at in these papers will materialize; others will have unanticipated downsides and will have to be abandoned. But it is nearly certain that some of these innovations will prove to be practical, cost-efficient, environmentally neutral, and responsible for significant increases in the world food supply.

Solutions for a Cultivated Planet

In 2011, *Nature* magazine published a series of articles on the topic "Solutions for a Cultivated Planet." These pieces took up exactly the questions that have occupied us in this chapter. "To meet the world's future food security and sustainability needs, food production must grow substantially while, at the same time, agriculture's environmental footprint must shrink dramatically" (p. 337). Rather than despair that the situation is hopeless, these articles review a series of steps that, if taken, would approximately double global food production with minimal environmental impact. These strategies include "halting agricultural expansion, closing 'yield gaps' on underperforming lands, increasing cropping efficiency, shifting diets and reducing waste."

First, the portion of ice-free land devoted to agricultural has increased in recent decades but mainly to grow animal feed and biofuel stocks. Much of this land has become available through deforestation, which has had large negative environmental impacts. If our dependence on biofuels is going to increase, alternatives to corn and soy feed stocks must be developed. Waste biomass is abundant and, while not as energy rich, is a more sustainable alternative than grain that could provide food for humans.

Second, "yield gaps" refer to the difference between "crop yields observed at any given location and the crop's potential yield at the same location given current agricultural practices and technologies" (p. 339), or the difference between maximum and observed productivity. These gaps are ubiquitous around the world and usually result from poor management. "Better deployment of existing crop varieties with improved management should be able to close many yield gaps, while continued improvements in crop genetics will probably increase potential yields into the future" (p. 339). Under aggressive but not unattainable assumptions, closing yield gaps alone could increase the global supply of food by over 50 percent.

Third, increased cropping efficiency mainly refers to the global use of nitrogen- and phosphorous-based fertilizers, which are applied more heavily than necessary in China, India, the United States, and western Europe and less heavily than necessary in much of the rest of the world. Solving the "Goldilocks" problem (not too much, not too little, just the right amount) would reduce environmental impacts in the "too much" regions and improve yields in the "too little" regions. Optimizing fertilizer use and distribution, coupled with better manure management and enhanced capture of excess nutrients through recycling, wetland restoration, and like measures, shows "great promise for improving the resource efficiency of agriculture, maintaining the benefits of intensive agriculture while greatly reducing harm to the environment" (p. 340).

Fourth, meat, especially beef, is the most resource-consumptive item in the human diet, so if people could be persuaded to eat less meat or to switch from beef to chicken and pork, the potential net global food savings could be substantial. A related change would be pasture-fed rather than grain-fed animals. The authors of the *Nature* series acknowledge, however, that "wholesale conversions of the human diet . . . are not realistic goals." Still, "even incremental steps could be extremely beneficial" (p. 5). Much of the potential savings could be realized by greater efficiencies in how meat animals are raised (what they are fed, how and when they are pastured, etc.) and these savings would be realized whether people were persuaded to eat less meat or not.

Fifth and finally, although estimates of the percentages vary, it is obvious that large amounts of food are wasted. Depending on study, focus, methodology, and other factors, waste is at least a third of the total yield and quite possibly half. Even once food gets to retail, is purchased, and brought into homes, as much as 40 percent goes to waste. Some waste is inevitable, of course, but strategies to reduce the volume of waste show great promise to increase the world food supply.

The Twenty-First-Century Peasantry

The Green Revolution is largely responsible for what is called industrial agriculture or, less charitably, factory farming. On the upside, factory farming has magnified yields many times over; on the downside, industrial agriculture has been an environmental disaster and has largely destroyed the family farm and farmer and, with them, the small-producer agrarian style of life. It can even be argued that "farmers" have disappeared. What we have instead are immensely large food factories covering thousands of acres, worked largely by mechanical devices consuming fossil fuels and operated by semiskilled machine tenders, producing mostly a supply of industrial feedstock that is turned into cloth, biofuels, oil, plastics, building materials, adhesives, solvents, animal feed, and (more or less incidentally) human food. Farming as it was traditionally understood has largely disappeared from modern urban-industrial life. Or has it?

Dutch rural sociologist Jan Van der Ploeg has argued that this depiction is an exaggeration and that we are presently witnessing a "repeasantization"—that is, "reversing the once seemingly inevitable processes of modernization and urbanization" (2015:664). This is occurring through six mechanisms "that together have a strong impact on the nature and dynamics of the process of agricultural development." Being a peasant (a small agricultural producer) has always been about more than being involved in agriculture. Peasantry implies "a livelihood that provides [peasants] with employment, income, an identity, a place to belong to (which is also a relatively safe and clean space for their children to grow up), social networks, and, probably, some level of dignity and the feeling that they are part of a more comprehensive whole" (p. 664). For much of the world, "peasantry is the only realistic alternative" to miserable slums in the global cities. "Farming-as-a-livelihood" is what is being driven off by industrial agriculture, so a twenty-first-century peasantry is an anachronism.

However, peasant agriculture embraces many of the principles that ecologists and food activists favor: ecological rather than industrial "intensification" and the substitution of labor for capital (instead of the reverse). So perhaps "repeasantization" can contribute to sustainable intensification after all. Van der Ploeg's argument is that contrary to expectations, the peasantry is not only surviving but also thriving and that peasants can be and will be a continuing presence in global agriculture for the foreseeable future:

> Peasant agriculture has the potential to be highly productive and efficient. Its yields are often considerably higher than those from other forms of agricultural production, and its output-to-input ratios reflect high levels of efficiency. In addition, peasant farming creates much employment and generates considerable incomes, thus contributing to the enlargement of the domestic (and particularly

rural) market (which in turn may trigger other forms of economic growth. It can be a safeguard for sustainability and contribute to the emancipation of downtrodden social groups in society. Equally it plays a strong role in safeguarding biodiversity, scenic landscapes, and the attractiveness and accessibility of the countryside as a whole. (p. 664)

The peasantry has figured out a great deal that industrial agriculture has overlooked, forgotten, or ignored. Do the world's small agricultural producers therefore have a significant role to play in satisfying the global demand for food? Apparently yes, for six reasons.

Reducing External Inputs

External agricultural inputs were essential to the success of the Green Revolution, and nearly all of them replaced internal (farm-based) inputs. Chemical fertilizers replaced manure and soil nurturing; industrially processed feed and additives replaced locally grown hay and fodder; hand weeding was replaced by herbicides. Initially, the result was vast increases in yield. But these inputs are expensive and many farmers went into debt to stay competitive. In time, the cost of acquiring these external inputs represented an ever-greater proportion of total farm income.

With their existence threatened, many farmers "are returning to their neglected internal resources, trying to upgrade their quality, and simultaneously reduce the use of costly external inputs" (Van der Ploeg 2015:665). Not coincidentally, this also wrests control of the farm away from agrarian scientists and their "scripts" of success and returns control to local knowledge. The result is a net increase in yield and a lessening of environmental impacts.

A case in point is the European rediscovery of manure. Prior to the Green Revolution, manure was recycled into the fields. The Green Revolution turned this valuable phosphorous- and nitrogen-rich soil conditioner into a troublesome waste product that fouled the air, polluted the soil, and degraded local waterways. Presently, European farmers are "once again rebuilding manure into a highly valuable internal input, to replace chemical fertilizers. This is done through a range of ingenious adaptations, including the dietary regime of the animals, the storage of the manure, the use of straw in the cowsheds, and the way manure is spread on the fields" (p. 665). Similar trends are observed in Central and South America.

Multifunctionality

Factory farms tend to have a single function, which is producing raw materials (corn, soy, cotton, wheat) for agro-industrial applications. Some of the product is food for humans but a great deal is not. The modern peasantry produces food and a host of new services and products that increase income and make the farm a going economic concern. "The other functions of a farm can include energy production, water retention, the management of nature and landscape, increasing or safeguarding biodiversity, agritourism, afforestation, fish ponds, care facilities, and a range of classical forms of diversification" (Van der Ploeg 2015:665). Such trends are evident throughout Europe and China and have also begun to take hold in Brazil, Chile, and even North America. Many small farms in North America have become agricultural boutiques, producing organic food, exotic vegetables and fruits, other specialty items, herbs, heirloom agricultural products, and other high-profit commodities. Small farmers make good profits on these diversifications because the demand, while small, is insistent and largely price-inelastic—they satisfy demand niches that industrial agriculture would never touch.

Multiple Job-Holding

Even under favorable circumstances, it can be difficult to wrest an adequate living from farming, so worldwide, peasant agriculture has become mainly a part-time job, and multiple job-holding is the norm. A recent study of Dutch dairy farms found that 85 percent of them had one or more adults working outside jobs that accounted for at least a third of total household income. "By embedding the farm in a larger portfolio of economic activities, within and beyond the farm, farm continuity and development become feasible" (Van der Ploeg 2015:666).

Retreat from Entrepreneurialism

"Entrepreneurial farming" is Van der Ploeg's term for what we have called factory farming. For many farmers, particularly small producers, industrial agriculture came to mean increased yields but also "indebtedness, high levels of environmental pollution, stagnating yields, and the unwillingness of [some] banks to continue their credit lines" (2015:667). Monocultural farming is highly vulnerable to fluctuating prices and global market conditions; the more varied production of peasant-style farms provides a cushion against unfavorable market forces. "At the symbolic level, the entrepreneurial model has lost much of its appeal and legitimacy. Meanwhile, the peasant way of farming is coming to be understood as a strong institution and possibly the best guarantee for food security and food sovereignty" (p. 667).

Enlarging the Ranks

The farm population of all advanced societies has steadily decreased for at least the past fifty years, but the numbers are increasing in the global South. One well-known example is Brazil's Movimento dos Sem Terra (Movement of Landless People), an organized effort to move huge numbers of slum dwellers out of the cities and into the undeveloped countryside to create new farms. Between Brazil's last two agricultural censuses (1996 and 2006), the number of peasant farms increased by more than 400,000. Similar efforts can be observed in the Mediterranean countries of Europe, in China, and elsewhere.

Countering Big Capital

"From a sociological point of view it is noteworthy that, for the first time in history, the world now has an organization, La Via Campesina (LVC, which translates as 'the peasant trajectory'), which has developed to become a truly global peasant federation. This is a well-coordinated agglomeration of many organizations and movements that operate at national, regional, and local levels. LVC gives a voice to those who would otherwise remain neglected in this world" (Van der Ploeg 2015:667). LVC resists land- and water-grabbing, advocates for agro-ecology, and defends smallholders "against big capital groups and their endeavors to conquer spaces and create new conditions for capital accumulation in the countryside" (p. 667). It is largely responsible for the so-called food sovereignty movement, "defined as the right of people to decide on how they want the production, processing, distribution, and consumption of food to be organized" (p. 667).

* * *

What we learn from this analysis is that many of the virtues of small farms and farmers can be retained even in an agricultural era dominated by factory farming; in some cases, the small farms are more productive than factory farms and have fewer environmental impacts. In some discussions, the issue is pitched as peasants *versus* industrial agriculture, as small farms *versus* factory farms, but the real lesson is that small- and large-scale agricultural production can coexist and doubtlessly will for the remainder of the twenty-first century.

Conclusion

Can the world continue to feed itself sustainably over the next half century? Or is Malthusian catastrophe just around the corner? The evidence does not allow a definitive conclusion, but there is ample reason for optimism. The principal problems are not technical or scientific but rather social and political.

Of the many possible futures, the most likely is vast increases in agricultural yield resulting from genetically engineered organisms. The technology for genetic engineering already exists and is rapidly developing, and the potential benefits are almost unimaginable. Here the roadblock is helping people conquer their fears of Big Science and their hesitance in the face of the unknown. Many GMO food products are already on the market and more are sure to follow. The idea that the GMO momentum can be halted is naive. The risks of not pursuing GMO solutions to the global food problem are surely greater than the risks of GMOs themselves.

As we have seen, food insecurity at all levels is less a problem of production than one of access and distribution, and this too will remain true. Compared to production, which on the preceding analysis will remain adequate into the indefinite future, little attention has been paid to access and distribution, perhaps because they do not lend themselves so readily to technological solutions. It is one thing to double maize production on Chinese farms (which turns out to be relatively simple) but quite another to get that surplus maize to remote rural villages in Guizhou province. If there is mass starvation in the next half century, it will not be because the people of the planet lacked food, but because we lacked courage and political will.

Amartya Sen (1981) says that people are "entitled" to food if they grow food themselves or have the cash to buy food from those who do. As an economic analysis, this perspective has been fruitful, but as a social or political proposition it is disastrous. People are "entitled" to food as a right of citizenship in the world community, and it is, or rather should be, the responsibility of governments to secure that right.

As we have seen in earlier chapters, most private- and public-sector efforts to address food insecurity in the United States have failed, largely because they ignore the implications of Sen's analysis—that providing income is a more equitable and efficient way to reduce food insecurity than providing food itself. Virtually everything the United States does to address the issue involves direct provision of food: the food pantries where needy families can go to acquire food, the home-delivery programs that bring food directly to homebound seniors, the school feeding programs, even SNAP benefits that can be used to purchase only food (and even then, only prescribed food items). Overlooked in all of this is the fundamental point that food insecurity is a poverty problem and will be solved only once the larger poverty issue is solved.

Alas, eliminating poverty (or even significantly reducing it) is not a popular item on anyone's political agenda, least of all in the United States, where it is still insisted that people are poor mainly because they are lazy and are content to get by on the dole. For this reason, and using standard measures, there are proportionally more people in poverty in the United States than in Belgium, Sweden, the United Kingdom, France, Denmark, Indonesia, Austria, Norway, Ireland, and a score of other advanced nations.[1] The American poor are roughly 15 percent of the national population, and the United States will struggle with issues of hunger and food insecurity as long as this remains true.

Food activist Mark Winne (2008) has written extensively about his struggles to provide healthy, affordable food to the urban poor in Hartford, Connecticut, and in this connection he comments at length on the abandonment by the US government of its goals to reduce poverty in the United States. The federal government today, he notes, is less concerned about the poor and their access to food than about farmers' access to deep agricultural subsidies that keep farming profitable.

More than 90 percent of all SNAP benefits go to households with dependent children, seniors, or disabled people. Very few SNAP beneficiaries are able-bodied adults of working age who could "work if they want to." This fact has been well-known for more than a decade but is routinely overlooked or ignored each time SNAP comes up for reauthorization. Likewise, one finds no affluent suburban housewives in the food pantries of Central Florida trying to score a free can of green beans or a few boxes of macaroni and cheese. Indeed, if one spends time volunteering in these pantries, as all of the authors of this book have done, the overwhelming impression one comes away with is that these are people ground down by a social, political, and economic system that considers them subhuman, as barely worthy of assistance, much less deserving of what shards of charity they receive.

Few people these days remember Hubert Humphrey, a senator from Minnesota, vice president to Lyndon Baines Johnson, and the unsuccessful 1968 Democratic candidate for the presidency. Humphrey died in 1978 and gave his last speech at the dedication of the Hubert H. Humphrey Building (which now serves as the home of the US Department of Health and Human Services). The most memorable and oft-quoted line from that speech is that "the moral test of government is how that government treats those who are in the dawn of life, the children; those who are in the twilight of life, the elderly; those who are in the shadows of life, the sick, the needy and the handicapped." The continued presence of poverty and food insecurity in the United States makes this a test the government has failed.

Note

1. According to the table of data at https://www.indexmundi.com/g/r.aspx?v=69.

Appendix:
Survey Questions Used by the USDA to Assess Household Food Security

1. "We worried whether our food would run out before we got money to buy more." Was that often, sometimes, or never true for you in the last 12 months?
     Often true [4.9 percent]
     Sometimes true [13.9 percent]
     Never true [81.2 percent]

2. "The food that we bought just didn't last and we didn't have money to get more." Was that often, sometimes, or never true for you in the last 12 months?
     Often true [3.4 percent]
     Sometimes true [12.2 percent]
     Never true [84.4 percent]

3. "We couldn't afford to eat balanced meals." Was that often, sometimes, or never true for you in the last 12 months?
     Often true [3.8 percent]
     Sometimes true [11.0 percent]
     Never true [85.2 percent]

4. In the last 12 months, did you or other adults in the household ever cut the size of your meals or skip meals because there wasn't enough money for food? (Yes/No)

155

Yes [8.6 percent]

No [91.4 percent]

5. (If yes to question 4) How often did this happen—almost every month, some months but not every month, or in only 1 or 2 months?

Almost every month [3.0 percent of all households or 35 percent of those who answered Yes to question 4]

Some months but not every month [3.7 percent of all households or 43 percent of those who answered Yes to question 4]

In only 1 or 2 months [1.9 percent of all households or 22 percent of those who answered Yes to question 4]

6. In the last 12 months, did you ever eat less than you felt you should because there wasn't enough money for food? (Yes/No)

Yes [8.8 percent]

No [91.2 percent]

7. In the last 12 months, were you ever hungry, but didn't eat, because there wasn't enough money for food? (Yes/No)

Yes [4.4 percent]

No [95.6 percent]

8. In the last 12 months, did you lose weight because there wasn't enough money for food? (Yes/No)

Yes [2.9 percent]

No [97.1 percent]

9. In the last 12 months did you or other adults in your household ever not eat for a whole day because there wasn't enough money for food? (Yes/No)

Yes [1.7 percent]

No [98.3 percent]

10. (If yes to question 9) How often did this happen—almost every month, some months but not every month, or in only 1 or 2 months?

Almost every month [0.6 percent of all households or 35 percent of those who answered Yes to question 9]

Some months but not every month [0.7 percent of all households or 40 percent of those who answered Yes to question 9]

In only 1 or 2 months [0.4 percent of all households or 25 percent of those who answered Yes to question 9]

(Questions 11–18 are asked if the household includes children age 0–17.)

11. "We relied on only a few kinds of low-cost food to feed our children because we were running out of money to buy food." Was that often, sometimes, or never true for you in the last 12 months?
    Often true [3.6 percent]
    Sometimes true [12.7 percent]
    Never true [83.7 percent]

12. "We couldn't feed our children a balanced meal, because we couldn't afford that." Was that often, sometimes, or never true for you in the last 12 months?
    Often true [1.8 percent]
    Sometimes true [8.2 percent]
    Never true [90 percent]

13. "The children were not eating enough because we just couldn't afford enough food." Was that often, sometimes, or never true for you in the last 12 months?
    Often true [0.7 percent]
    Sometimes true [3.6 percent]
    Never true [95.7 percent]

14. In the last 12 months, did you ever cut the size of any of the children's meals because there wasn't enough money for food? (Yes/No)
    Yes [2.3 percent]
    No [97.7 percent]

15. In the last 12 months, were the children ever hungry but you just couldn't afford more food? (Yes/No)
    Yes [1.3 percent]
    No [98.7 percent]

16. In the last 12 months, did any of the children ever skip a meal because there wasn't enough money for food? (Yes/No)
    Yes [0.8 percent]
    No [99.2 percent]

17. (If yes to question 16) How often did this happen—almost every month, some months but not every month, or in only 1 or 2 months?

> Almost every month [0.2 percent of all households or 30 percent of those who said Yes to question 16]

> Some months but not every month [0.3 percent of all households or 42 percent of those who said Yes to question 16]

> In only 1 or 2 months [0.2 percent of all households or 28 percent of those who said Yes to question 16]

18. In the last 12 months did any of the children ever not eat for a whole day because there wasn't enough money for food? (Yes/No)

> Yes [0.2 percent]
> No [99.8 percent]

Source: Coleman-Jenson, Gregory, and Singh 2014.

References

Acheampong, Irene, and Lauren Haldeman. 2013. "Are Nutrition Knowledge, Attitudes, and Beliefs Associated with Obesity Among Low-Income Hispanic and African-American Women Caretakers?" *Journal of Obesity.* http://dx.doi.org/10.1155/2013/123901.

Aggarwal, Anju, Andrea J. Cook, Junfeng Jiao, Rebecca A. Seguin, Anne Vernez Moudon, Philip M. Hurvitz, and Adam Drewnowski. 2014. "Access to Supermarkets and Fruit and Vegetable Consumption." *American Journal of Public Health* 104:917–923.

Alkon, Alison Hope. 2012. *Black, White, and Green: Farmers Markets, Race, and the Green Economy.* Athens: University of Georgia Press.

Alwitt, Linda F., and Thomas D. Donley. 1997. "Retail Stores in Poor Urban Neighborhoods." *Journal of Consumer Affairs* 31(1):139–164.

Anderson, Molly D., and John T. Cook. 1999. "Community Food Security: Practice in Need of Theory?" *Agriculture and Human Values* 16(2):141–150.

Andrews, Margaret, Rhea Bhatta, and Michele Ver Ploeg. 2013. "An Alternative to Developing Stores in Food Deserts: Can Changes in SNAP Benefits Make a Difference?" *Applied Economic Perspectives and Policy* 35(1):150–170.

Andrews, Margaret, Gary Bickel, and Steven Carlson. 1998. "Household Food Security in the United States in 1995: Results From the Food Security Measurement Project." *Family Economics and Nutrition Review* 11(1–2):17–28.

Andrews, Margaret, and David Smallwood. 2012. "What's Behind the Rise in SNAP Participation?" *Amber Waves,* March. https://www.ers.usda.gov/amber-waves/2012/march/what-s-behind-the-rise-in-snap-participation.

Andreyeva, Tatiana, Amanda S. Tripp, and Marlene B. Schwartz. 2015. "Dietary Quality of Americans by SNAP Participation Status: A Systematic Review." *American Journal of Preventive Medicine* 49(4):594–604.

Armstrong, Donna. 2000. "A Survey of Community Gardens in Upstate New York: Implications for Health Promotion and Community Development." *Health & Place* 6:319–327.

Asperin, Amelia Estepa, Mary Frances Nettles, and Deborah Carr. 2008. "Exploring Factors That Affect the School Lunch Experience of High School Students." Technical Report no. R-147-09. University, Miss.: National Food Service Management Institute. http://www.nfsmi.org/documentlibraryfiles /PDF/20090910084551.pdf.

Bailey-Davis, Lisa, Amy Virus, Tara Alexis McCoy, Alexis Wojtanowski, Stephanie S. Vander Veur, and Gary D. Foster. 2013. "Middle School Student and Parent Perceptions of Government-Sponsored Free School Breakfast and Consumption: A Qualitative Inquiry in an Urban Setting." *Journal of the Academy of Nutrition and Dietetics* 113:251–257.

Baker, Lauren E. 2004. "Tending Cultural Landscapes and Food Citizenship in Toronto's Community Gardens." *Geographical Review* 94(3):305–325.

Berg, Nathan, and James Murdoch. 2008. "Access to Grocery Stores in Dallas." *International Journal of Behavioural and Healthcare Research* 1:22–37.

Berkowitz, Seth A., Hilary K. Seligman, and Niteesh K. Choudhry. 2014. "Treat or Eat: Food Insecurity, Cost-Related Medication Underuse, and Unmet Needs." *American Journal of Medicine* 127:303–310.

Bernal, Jennifer, Edward A. Frongillo, Héctor A. Herrera, and Juan A. Rivera. 2014. "Food Insecurity in Children but Not in Their Mothers Is Associated with Altered Activities, School Absenteeism, and Stunting." *Journal of Nutrition* 144(10):1619–1626.

Bhatia, Rajiv, Paula Jones, and Zetta Reicker. 2011. "Competitive Foods, Discrimination, and Participation in the National School Lunch Program." *American Journal of Public Health* 101(8):1380–1386.

Bianchi, Suzanne M., Reynolds Farley, and Daphne Spain. 1982. "Racial Inequalities in Housing: An Examination of Recent Trends." *Demography* 19(1):37–51.

Bien, Angela, Jamille Bigio, Eric Buchner, Christine Compton, Rachel Markus, Ellen Massey, Stephen Mihalcik, and Michael Soracoe. 2004. "Physical and Mental Well-Being in Urban and Rural Communities: Impact of Non-Medical Factors on Limited Resource Families." Maryland Family Policy Impact Seminar. https://sph.umd.edu/sites/default/files/files/Gemstonebrief7-13-04.pdf.

Biros, Michelle H., Pamela L. Hoffman, and Karen Resch. 2005. "The Prevalence and Perceived Consequences of Hunger in Emergency Department Patient Populations." *Academic Emergency Medicine* 12:310–317.

Bitler, Marianne. 2014. "The Health and Nutrition Effects of SNAP: Selection into the Program and a Review of the Literature on Its Effects." University of Kentucky Center for Poverty Research Discussion Paper Series. http:// www.ukcpr.org/Publications/DP2014-02.pdf.

Black, Rachel. 2013. "Taking Space to Grow Food and Community: Urban Agriculture and Guerrilla Gardening in Vancouver." *Cuizine* 4(1). https://www .erudit.org/revue/cuizine/2013/v4/n1/1015492ar.html.

Bommarco, Riccardo, David Kleijn, and Simon G. Potts. 2013. "Ecological Intensification: Harnessing Ecosystem Services for Food Security." *Trends in Ecology and Evolution* 28:230–238.

Boone-Heinonen, Janne, Penny Gordon-Larsen, Catarina I. Kiefe, James M. Shikany, Cora E. Lewis, and Barry M. Popkin. 2011. "Fast Food Restaurants and Food Stores Associations with Diet in Young to Middle-Aged Adults: The CARDIA Study." *Archives of Internal Medicine* 171(13):1162–1170.

Bowens, Natasha. 2015. *The Color of Food: Stories of Race, Resilience, and Farming*. Gabriola, Canada: New Society.

Bradford, Jason. 2012. "One Acre Feeds a Person." http://www.farmlandlp.com /2012/01/one-acre-feeds-a-person.

Brauman, Kate A., Stefan Siebert, and Jonathan A. Foley. 2013. "Improvements in Crop Water Productivity Increase Water Sustainability and Food Security—A Global Analysis." *Environmental Research Letters.* http://dx.doi.org /10.1088/1748-9326/8/2/024030.

Brewer, Dawn P., Christina S. Catlett, Katie N. Porter, Jung S. Lee, Dorothy B. Hausman, Sudha Reddy, and Mary A. Johnson. 2010. "Physical Limitations Contribute to Food Insecurity and the Food Insecurity-Obesity Paradox in Older Adults at Senior Centers in Georgia." *Journal of Nutrition for the Elderly* 29:150–169.

Bridges, Jeff. 2010. "Excerpt from Luncheon Address to the National Press Club." http://www.press.org/events/npc-luncheon-jeff-bridges.

Broad, Garret. 2016. *More Than Just Food: Food Justice and Community Change.* Berkeley: University of California Press.

Bruenig, Matt. 2012. "Confusion Around Food Deserts." http://mattbruenig.com /2012/04/14/confusion-around-food-deserts.

Bullis, Kevin. 2015. "Supercharged Photosynthesis." *MIT Technology Review 2015.* http://www.technologyreview.com/featuredstory/535011/supercharged -photosynthesis.

Callum-Penso, Lillia. 2014. "Convenience Stores Discover New Food Trend." *Greenville News,* July 15. http://www.thestate.com/living/article13868492.html.

Canadian Office of Nutrition Policy and Promotion. 2007. *Income-Related Household Food Security in Canada.* http://www.hc-sc.gc.ca/fn-an/surveill /nutrition/commun/income_food_sec-sec_alim-eng.php.

Carlson, Steven J., Margaret S. Andrews, and Gary W. Bickel. 1999. "Measuring Food Insecurity and Hunger in the United States: Development of a National Benchmark Measure and Prevalence Estimates." *Journal of Nutrition* 129(2):510S–516S.

Castillo, Alexandra, and Kristi L. Lofton. 2012. "Development of Middle/Junior High School Student Surveys to Measure Factors That Impact Participation in and Satisfaction with the National School Lunch Program." University, Miss.: National Food Service Management Institute. http://www.nfsmi.org /documentlibraryfiles/PDF/20120402024129.pdf.

Castillo, Alexandra, Kristi L. Lofton, and Mary Frances Nettles. 2011. "Determining Factors Impacting the Decision of Middle/Junior High School Students to Participate in the National School Lunch Program." University, Miss.: National Food Service Management Institute. http://www.nfsmi.org /documentlibraryfiles/PDF/20140217013125.pdf.

Center on Budget and Policy Priorities. 2015. "Policy Basics: Introduction to the Supplemental Nutrition Assistance Program (SNAP)." http://www.cbpp.org /research/policy-basics-introduction-to-the-supplemental-nutrition-assistance -program-snap.

Chakraborty, Swati, and Adrian Clive Newton. 2011. "Climate Change, Plant Diseases, and Food Security: An Overview." *Plant Pathology* 60:2–14.

Champagne, Catherine M., Patrick H. Casey, Carol L. Connell, Janice E. Stuff, Jeffrey M. Gossett, David W. Harsha, Beverly McCabe-Sellers, James M. Robbins, Pippa M. Simpson, Judith L. Weber, and Margaret L. Bogle. 2007. "Poverty and Food Intake in Rural America: Diet Quality Is Lower in Food Insecure Adults in the Mississippi Delta." *Journal of the American Dietetic Association* 107(11):1886–1894.

Chen, Xin-Ping, Zhen-Ling Cui, Peter M. Vitousek, Kenneth G. Cassman, Pamela A. Matson, Jin-Shun Bai, Qing-Feng Meng, Peng Hou, Shan-Chao Yue, Volker Römheld, and Fu-Suo Zhanga. 2011. "Integrated Soil-Crop System Management for Food Security." *Proceedings of the National Academy of Sciences of the United States of America* 108(16):6399–6404.

Chilton, Mariana, Jenny Rabinowich, Amanda Breen, and Sherita Mouzon. 2013. "When the Systems Fail: Individual and Household Coping Strategies Related to Child Hunger." https://sites.nationalacademies.org/cs/groups /dbassesite/documents/webpage/dbasse_084305.pdf.

Chumley, Cheryl K. 2013. "Kentucky Kids to First Lady Michelle Obama: Your Food 'Tastes Like Vomit.'" *Washington Times,* August 28. http://www .washingtontimes.com/news/2013/aug/28/kentucky-kids-first-lady-your -food-tastes-vomit.

Clancy, Katherine, Jean Bowering, and Janet Poppendieck. 1989. "Use of Emergency Feeding Systems in New York State." Presentation at annual meeting of the American Public Health Association, Chicago, October 24.

Clark, Krissy. 2014. "The Secret Life of a Food Stamp." Slate April 1, 2014. http://www.slate.com/articles/business/moneybox/2014/04/big_box_stores _make_billions_off_food_stamps_often_it_s_their_own_workers.html.

Cluss Patricia A., Linda Ewing, Wendy C. King, Evelyn Cohen Reis, Judith L. Dodd, and Barbara Penner. 2013. "Nutrition Knowledge of Low-Income Parents of Obese Children." *Translational Behavioral Medicine* 3(2):218–225.

Cohen, Juliana F. W., Scott Richardson, S. Bryn Austin, Christina D. Economos, and Eric B. Rimm. 2013. "School Lunch Waste Among Middle School Students: Nutrients Consumed and Costs." *American Journal of Preventive Medicine* 44(2):114–121.

Colello, Kirsten J. 2011. "Older Americans Act: Title III Nutrition Services Program." http://nationalaglawcenter.org/wp-content/uploads/assets/crs/RS21202.pdf.

Coleman-Jensen, Alisha. 2010. "U.S. Food Insecurity Status: Toward a Refined Definition." *Social Indicators Research* 95:215–230.

Coleman-Jensen, Alisha, Christian Gregory, and Anita Singh. 2014. "Household Food Security in the United States in 2013." USDA Economic Research Service.

Condon, Elizabeth, Susan Drilea, Keri Jowers, Carolyn Lichtenstein, James Mabli, Emily Madden, and Katherine Niland. 2015. "Diet Quality of Americans by SNAP Participation Status: Data from the National Health and Nutrition Examination Survey, 2007–2010." Food and Nutrition Service, US Department of Agriculture. http://www.fns.usda.gov/sites/default/files/ops /NHANES-SNAP07-10.pdf.

Cordell, Dana, and Stuart White. 2014. "Life's Bottleneck: Sustaining the World's Phosphorus for a Food Secure Future." *Annual Review of Environment and Resources* 39:161–188.

Cummins, Steven, and Sally Macintyre. 1999. "The Location of Food Stores in Urban Areas: A Case Study in Glasgow." *British Food Journal* 101(7):545–553.

Cummins, Steven, Ellen Flint, and Stephen A. Matthews. 2014. "New Neighborhood Grocery Store Increased Awareness of Food Access but Did Not Alter Dietary Habits or Obesity." *Health Affairs* 33(2):283–291.

Davis, Brennan, and Christopher Carpenter. 2009. "Proximity of Fast-Food Restaurants to Schools and Adolescent Obesity." *American Journal of Public Health* 99(3):505–510.

Dean, Stacy. 2008. "Strengthening the Food Stamp Program to Serve Low-Income Seniors." Center on Budget and Policy Priorities. https://www.cbpp.org/sites/default/files/atoms/files/3-5-08fa.pdf.

Delaney, Arthur. 2013. "Food Stamps Avoided by Millions of Eligible Americans." *Huffington Post,* August 1. http://www.huffingtonpost.com/2013/08/01/food-stamp-cuts_n_3691093.html.

Des Moines Register. 2015. "Editorial: Stop Demonizing Americans Using Food Assistance." September 18. http://www.desmoinesregister.com/story/opinion/editorials/caucus/2015/09/18/editorial-stop-demonizing-americans-using-food-assistance/32501439.

Devine, Joel A., Mark Plunkett, and James D. Wright. 1992. "The Chronicity of Poverty: Evidence from the PSID, 1968–1987." *Social Forces* 70(3):787–812.

Diallo, Mamadou S., and C. Jeffrey Brinker. 2011. "Nanotechnology for Sustainability: Environment, Water, Food, Minerals, and Climate." In Mark Hersham, M. C. Roco, and Chad A. Mirkin (eds.), *Nanotechnology Research Directions for Societal Needs in 2020: Retrospective and Outlook,* 221–259. Dordrecht: Springer.

Diesenhouse, Susan. 1993. "As Suburbs Slow, Supermarkets Return to the Cities." *New York Times,* June 27.

Ding, Meng, Margaret K. Keiley, Kimberly B. Garza, Patricia A. Duffy, and Claire A. Zizza. 2015. "Food Insecurity Is Associated with Poor Sleep Outcomes Among US Adults." *Journal of Nutrition* 145(3):615–621.

Dinour, Lauren M., Dara Bergen, and Ming-Chin Yeh. 2007. "The Food Insecurity–Obesity Paradox: A Review of the Literature and the Role Food Stamps May Play." *Journal of the American Dietetic Association* 107(11): 1952–1961.

Donley, Amy, and Marie Gualtieri. 2015. "Food Deserts." In James D. Wright (ed.), *The International Encyclopedia of the Social and Behavioral Sciences,* 2nd ed., volume 9, pp. 285–289. Oxford: Elsevier.

Draper, Carrie, and Darcy Freedman. 2010. "Review and Analysis of the Benefits, Purposes, and Motivations Associated with Community Gardening in the United States." *Journal of Community Practice* 18(4):458–492.

Drewnowski, Adam. 2009. "Obesity, Diets, and Social Inequalities." *Nutrition Review* 67:S36–S39.

Drewnowski, Adam, Anju Aggarwal, and Anne Vemez Moudon. 2010. "The Supermarket Gap: How to Ensure Equitable Access to Affordable, Healthy Foods." Research brief. University of Washington Center of Public Health Nutrition. http://depts.washington.edu/uwcphn/pubs/reports.shtml.

Dubowitz, Tamara, Shannon N. Zenk, Bonnie Ghosh-Dastidar, Deborah A. Cohen, Robin Beckman, Gerald Hunter, Elizabeth D. Steiner, and Rebecca L. Collins. 2014. "Healthy Food Access for Urban Food Desert Residents: Examination of the Food Environment, Food Purchasing Practices, Diet, and BMI." *Public Health Nutrition* 18(12):2220–2230.

The Economist. 2011. "Food Deserts: If You Build It, They May Not Come." July 7. http://www.economist.com/node/18929190.

Elbel, Brian, Alyssa Moran, L. Beth Dixon, Kamila Kiszko, Jonathan Cantor, Courtney Abrams, and Tod Mijanovicha. 2015. "Assessment of a Government-Subsidized Supermarket in a High-Need Area on Household Food Availability and Children's Dietary Intakes." *Public Health Nutrition* 18(15):2881–2890.

Falk, Gene, and Randy A. Aussenberg. 2014. "The Supplemental Nutrition Assistance Program (SNAP): Categorical Eligibility." https://fas.org/sgp/crs/misc/R42054.pdf.

Fields, Tanya. 2013. "The South Bronx: In a Food Desert Comes a Mobile Market Oasis." http://civileats.com/2013/04/16/the-south-bronx-in-a-food-desert-comes-a-mobile-market-oasis.

Flegal, Katherine M., Margaret D. Carroll, Brian K. Kit, and Cynthia L. Ogden. 2012. "Prevalence of Obesity and Trends in the Distribution of Body Mass Index Among US Adults, 1999–2010." *Journal of the American Medical Association* 307(5):491–497.

Florida Impact. 2014. "A Good Start for Learning: School Breakfast Participation in Florida, 2012–2013 School Year." http://www.flimpact.org/downloads/docs/2014-SchoolBreakfastParticipation-SY1213.pdf.

Florida School Breakfast Program. 2011. "Spotlight on Breakfast Success! Alternative Breakfast Models in Florida: Orange County Public Schools." http://floridaschoolbreakfast.org/resources/2013-Success_OrangeV2.pdf.

Flournoy, Rebecca. 2006. "Healthy Foods, Strong Communities." National Housing Institute. http://www.nhi.org/online/issues/147/healthyfoods.html.

Fogler-Levitt, Elizabeth, Daisy Lau, Adele Csima, Magdalena Krondl, and Patricia Coleman. 1995. "Utilization of Home-Delivered Meals by Recipients 75 Years of Age or Older." *Journal of the American Dietetic Association* 95:552–557.

Food Research and Action Center. 2010. "Seniors and SNAP/Food Stamps." http://frac.org/initiatives/addressing-senior-hunger/seniors-and-snapfood-stamps.

———. 2015. "National School Lunch Program: Trends and Factors Affecting Student Participation." http://frac.org/pdf/national_school_lunch_report_2015.pdf.

Franco, Angelo. 2015. "Are 'Food Deserts' a Myth or Simply Misidentified?" *Highbrow Magazine,* June 8. http://www.highbrowmagazine.com/5054-are-food-deserts-myth-or-simply-misidentified.

Franklin, Brandi, Ashley Jones, Dejuan Love, Stephane Puckett, Justin Macklin, and Shelley White-Means. 2012. "Exploring Mediators of Food Insecurity and Obesity: A Review of Recent Literature." *Journal of Community Health* 37(1):253–264.

Frongillo, Edward A., and Claire M. Horan. 2004. "Hunger and Aging." *Generations* 28(3):28–33.

Frongillo, Edward A., Tanushree D. Isaacman, Claire M. Horan, Elaine Wethington, and Karl Pillemer. 2010. "Adequacy of and Satisfaction with Delivery and Use of Home-Delivered Meals." *Journal of Nutrition for the Elderly* 29:211–226.

Frongillo, Edward A., and Wendy S. Wolfe. 2010. "Impact of Participation in Home-Delivered Meals on Nutrient Intake, Dietary Patterns, and Food Insecurity of Older Persons in New York State." *Journal of Nutrition for the Elderly* 29(3):293–310.

Frongillo, Edward A., Jr., Christine M. Olson, Barbara S. Rauschenbach, and Anne Kendall. 1997. "Nutritional Consequences of Food Insecurity in a Rural New York State County." Institute for Research on Poverty Discussion Paper no. 1120-97. http://irp.wisc.edu/publications/dps/pdfs/dp112097.pdf.

Gallagher, Mari. 2006. "Examining the Impact of Food Deserts on Public Health in Chicago." http://marigallagher.com/site_media/dynamic/project_files/1_ChicagoFoodDesertReport-Full_.pdf.

Geiger, Jennifer R., Scott E. Wilks, and Michelle M. Livermore. 2014. "Predicting SNAP Participation in Older Adults: Do Age Categorizations Matter?" *Educational Gerontology* 40:932–946.

Genuis, Shelagh K., Noreen Willows, Alexander First Nation, and Cindy G. Jardine. 2015. "Through the Lens of our Cameras: Children's Lived Experience with Food Security in a Canadian Indigenous Community." *Child Care Health and Development* 41:600–610.

Gleason, Philip M. 1995. "Participation in the National School Lunch Program and the School Breakfast Program." *American Journal of Clinical Nutrition* 61(1):213S–220S.

Godfray, H. Charles J., John R. Beddington, Ian R. Crute, Lawrence Haddad, David Lawrence, James F. Muir, Jules Pretty, Sherman Robinson, Sandy M. Thomas, and Camilla Toulmin. 2010. "Food Security: The Challenge of Feeding 9 Billion People." *Science* 327:812–820.

Government Accounting Office (GAO). 2013. "School Lunch: Modifications Needed to Some of the New Nutrition Standards." http://www.gao.gov/products /GAO-13-708T.

Grauerholz, Liz, and Nicole Owens. 2015. "Alternative Food Movements." In James D. Wright (ed.), *The International Encyclopedia of the Social and Behavioral Sciences,* 2nd ed., volume 1, 566–572. Oxford: Elsevier.

Greenlee, Kathy. 2011. "Statement on Senior Hunger and the Older Americans Act Before Committee on Health, Education, Labor, and Pensions Subcommittee on Primary Health and Aging United States Senate." http://www.hhs .gov/asl/testify/2011/06/t20110621a.html.

Gregory, Christian A., and Partha Deb. 2015. "Does SNAP Improve Your Health?" *Food Policy* 50:11–19.

"Grocery Store Development." 2012. http://www.kintera.org/ atf/cf/%7B97c6d565 -bb43-406d-a6d5-eca3bbf35af0%7D/GroceryStoreDevelopment.pdf.

Gualtieri, Marie, and Amy Donley. 2016. "Senior Hunger: The Importance of Quality Assessment Tools in Determining Need." *Journal of Applied Social Science* 10(1):8–21.

Gualtieri, Marie C., Amy M. Donley, James D. Wright, and Sara Strickhouser. 2018. "Home Delivered Meals to Seniors: A Critical Review of the Literature." *Home Healthcare Now* 36(3):159–168.

Gucciardi, Enza, Mandana Vahabi, Nicole Norris, John Paul Del Monte, and Cecile Farnum. 2014. "The Intersection Between Food Insecurity and Diabetes: A Review." *Current Nutrition Reports* 3(4):324–332.

Guitart, Daniela, Catherine Pickering, and Jason Byrne. 2012. "Past Results and Future Directions in Urban Community Gardens Research." *Urban Forestry and Urban Greening* 11:364–373.

Gupta, Palak, Kalyani Singh, Veenu Seth, Sidharth Agarwal, and Pulkit Mathur. 2015. "Coping Strategies Adopted by Households to Prevent Food Insecurity in Urban Slums of Delhi, India." *Journal of Food Security* 3(1):6–10.

Guthman, Julie. 2008. "'If They Only Knew': Color Blindness and Universalism in California Alternative Food Institutions." *Professional Geographer* 60(3):387–397.

———. 2011. "'If They Only Knew': The Unbearable Whiteness of Alternative Food." In Alison Hope Alkon and Julian Agyeman (eds.), *Cultivating Food Justice: Race, Class, and Sustainability,* 263–282. Boston: Massachusetts Institute of Technology Press.

Guthman, Julie, Amy W. Morris, and Patricia Allen. 2006. "Squaring Farm Security and Food Security in Two Types of Alternative Food Institutions." *Rural Sociology* 71(4):662–684.

Guy, Cliff, Graham Clarke, and Heather Eyre. 2004. "Food Retail Change and the Growth of Food Deserts: A Case Study of Cardiff." *International Journal of Retail and Distribution Management* 32(2):72–88.

Haas, Jessica, Leslie Cunningham-Sabo, and Garry Auld. 2014. "Plate Waste and Attitudes Among High School Lunch Program Participants." *Journal of Child Nutrition and Management* 38(1).

Hakim, Sharon M., and Gregory Meissen. 2013. "Increasing Consumption of Fruits and Vegetables in the School Cafeteria: The Influence of Active Choice." *Journal of Health Care for the Poor and Underserved* 24(2):145–157.

Hanson, Karla L., and Leah M. Connor. 2014. "Food Insecurity and Dietary Quality in US Adults and Children: A Systematic Review." *American Journal of Clinical Nutrition* 100(2):684–692.

Harrington, Deirdre M., Catherine M. Champagne, Stephanie T. Broyles, William D. Johnson, Catrine Tudor-Locke, and Peter T. Katzmarzyk. 2014. "Steps Ahead: A Randomized Trial to Reduce Unhealthy Weight Gain in the Lower Mississippi Delta." *Obesity* 22(5): E21–E28.

Hattori, Aiko, Ruopeng An, and Roland Sturm. 2013. "Neighborhood Food Outlets, Diet, and Obesity Among California Adults, 2007 and 2009." *Preventing Chronic Disease* 10:120–123.

Hendrickson, Deja, Chery Smith, and Nicole Eikenberry. 2006. "Fruit and Vegetable Access in Four Low-Income Food Deserts Communities in Minnesota." *Agriculture and Human Values* 23:371–383.

Hertwich, Edgar G., Ester van der Voet, Sangwon Suh, and Arnold Tukker. 2010. *Assessing the Environmental Impacts of Consumption and Production: Priority Products and Materials.* Nairobi: United Nations Environment Program.

Hewage, Sumali S. 2014. "The Relationship of Food Security, Cervical Health, and Produce Intake in Rural Appalachia." Master's thesis. https://etd.ohiolink.edu/!etd.send_file?accession=ohiou1397295968&disposition=inline.

Hilmers, Angela, Tzu-An Chen, Jayna M. Dave, Deborah Thompson, and Karen Weber Cullen. 2014. "Supplemental Nutrition Assistance Program Participation Did Not Help Low Income Hispanic Women in Texas Meet the Dietary Guidelines." *Preventative Medicine* 62:44–48.

Himmelgreen, David A., Rafael Perez-Escamilla, Sofia Segura-Millan, Yu-Kuei Peng, Anir Gonzalez, Merrill Singer, and Ann Ferris. 2000. "Food Insecurity Among Low-Income Hispanics in Hartford, Connecticut: Implications for Public Health Policy." *Human Organization* 59(3):334–342.

Hlubik, William T., Michael W. Hamm, Marc A. Winokur, and Monique V. Baron. 1994. "Incorporating Research with Community Gardens: The New Brunswick Community Gardening and Nutrition Program." In Mark Francis, Patricia Lindsey, and Jay Stone Rice (eds.), *The Healing Dimensions of People-Plant Relations: Proceedings of a Research Symposium,* 59–64. Davis: University of California–Davis, Department of Environmental Design, Center for Design Research.

Holben, David H. 2010. "Position of the American Dietetic Association: Food Insecurity in the United States." *Journal of the American Dietetic Association* 110(9):1368–1377.

Hook, Kristina. 2015. "Peace of Mind, Health of Body: Why the Correlation of Food Security, Physical Health, and Mental Wellbeing Holds Important Implications for Humanitarian Actors." *Journal of Humanitarian Assistance.* https://sites.tufts.edu/jha/archives/2115.

Huang, Jin, Karen Matta Oshima, and Youngmi Kim. 2010. "Does Food Insecurity Affect Parental Characteristics and Child Behavior? Testing Mediation Effects." *Social Service Review* 84(3):381–401.

Huang, Jin, and Michael G. Vaughn. 2015. "Household Food Insecurity and Children's Behaviour Problems: New Evidence from a Trajectories-Based Study." *British Journal of Social Work* 45(3):bcv033.

Hubbard, Rebecca R., Allison Palmberg, Janet Lydecker, Brooke Green, Nichole R. Kelly, Stephen Trapp, and Melanie K. Bean. 2016. "Culturally-Based Communication About Health, Eating and Food: Development and Validation of the CHEF Scale." *Appetite* 96(1):399–407.

Huet, Catherine, Roso Renata, and Grace M. Egeland. 2012. "The Prevalence of Food Insecurity Is High and the Diet Quality Poor in Inuit Communities." *Journal of Nutrition* 142(3):541–547.

"Hunger in America." 1968. CBS documentary. https://www.youtube.com/watch?v=h94bq4JfMAA.

Hutcheson, Graeme D., and Nick Sofroniou. 1999. *The Multivariate Social Scientist.* Thousand Oaks, Calif.: Sage.

Inglehart, Ronald. 1977. *The Silent Revolution: Changing Values and Political Styles Among Western Publics.* Princeton: Princeton University Press.

International Food Policy Research Institute. 2017. "Food Security." http://www.ifpri.org/topic/food-security.

Jacobs, Tom. 2015. "The Downside of Farmer's Markets." *The Week,* March 23. http://theweek.com/articles/544768/downside-farmers-markets.

Jones, Nicholas R. V., Annalijn I. Conklin, Marc Suhrcke, and Pablo Monsivais. 2014. "The Growing Price Gap Between More and Less Healthy Foods: Analysis of a Novel Longitudinal UK Dataset." *PLoS ONE.* http://dx.doi.org/10.1371/journal.pone.0109343.

Jones, Sonya J., and Edward A. Frongillo. 2006. "The Modifying Effects of Food Stamp Program Participation on the Relation Between Food Insecurity and Weight Change in Women." *Journal of Nutrition* 136(4):1091–1094.

Kato, Yuki. 2013. "Not Just the Price of Food: Challenges of an Urban Agriculture Organization in Engaging Local Residents." *Sociological Inquiry* 83(3):369–391.

Keller, Heather H. 2006. "Meal Programs Improve Nutritional Risk: A Longitudinal Analysis of Community-Living Seniors." *Journal of the American Dietetic Association* 106:1042–1048.

Kempson, Kathryn M., Debra Palmer Keenan, Puneeta Sonya Sadani, and Nancy Scotto Rosato. 2002. "Food Management Practices Used by People with Limited Resources to Maintain Food Sufficiency As Reported by Nutrition Educators." *Journal of the American Dietetic Association* 102(12):1795–1799.

Kendall, Anne, Christine M. Olson, and Edward A. Frongillo Jr. 1995. "Validation of the Radimer/Cornell Measures of Hunger and Food Insecurity." *Journal of Nutrition* 125:2793–2801.

———. 1996. "Relationship of Hunger and Food Insecurity to Food Availability and Consumption." *Journal of the American Dietetic Association* 96:1019–1024.

Kim, Kirang, and Edward A. Frongillo. 2007. "Participation in Food Assistance Programs Modifies the Relation of Food Insecurity with Weight and Depression in Elders." *Journal of Nutrition* 137:1005–1010.

Klesges, Lisa M., Marco Pahor, Ronald I. Shorr, Jim Y. Wan, Jeff D. Williamson, and Jack M. Guralnik. 2001. "Financial Difficulty in Acquiring Food Among

Elderly Disabled Women: Results from the Women's Health and Again Study." *American Journal of Public Health* 91:68–75.

Kortright, Robin, and Sarah Wakefield. 2011. "Edible Backyards: A Qualitative Study of Household Food Growing and Its Contributions to Food Security." *Agriculture and Human Values* 28(1):39–53.

Krassie, Jacquie G., Carmel Smart, and David C. K. Roberts. 2000. "A Review of the Nutritional Needs of Meals on Wheels Consumers and Factors Associated with the Provision of an Effective Meals on Wheels Service: An Australian Perspective." *European Journal of Clinical Nutrition* 54:275–280.

Krisberg, Kim. 2013. "New Study Confirms that Eating Healthy Does Indeed Cost More." *Pump Handle,* December 13. http://scienceblogs.com/thepumphandle/2013/12/13/new-study-confirms-that-eating-healthy-does-indeed-cost-more.

Lappé, Frances Moore, and Joseph Collins. 2015. *World Hunger: Ten Myths.* New York: Grove. Originally published in 1977.

Larchet, Nicholas, 2014. "Learning from the Corner Store: Food Reformers and the Black Urban Poor in a Southern US City." *Food, Culture, and Society* 17(5):395–416.

Lee, Helen. 2012. "The Role of Local Food Availability in Explaining Obesity Risk Among Young School-Aged Children." *Social Science and Medicine* 74:1193–1203.

Lee, Jung S., and Edward A. Frongillo. 2001. "Nutritional and Health Consequences Are Associated with Food Insecurity Among U.S. Elderly Persons." *Journal of Nutrition* 131:1503–1509.

Lee, Jung Sun, Edward A. Frongillo, Maria A. Keating, Lauren H. Deutsch, Jaclyn Daitchman, and Dominic E. Frongillo. 2008. "Targeting of Home-Delivered Meals Programs to Older Adults in the United States." *Journal of Nutrition for the Elderly* 27(3–4):405–415.

Lee, Kuei-I, and Rebecca Gould. 2012. "Predicting Congregate Meal Program Participation: Applying the Extended Theory of Planned Behavior." *International Journal of Hospitality Management* 31:828–836.

Leftin, Joshua, Esa Eslami, and Mark Strayer. 2011. "Trends in Supplemental Nutrition Assistance Program Participation Rates: 2002–2009." Alexandria, VA: Mathematica Policy Research for USDA Food and Nutrition Service.

Leung, Cindy W., Sarah Cluggish, Eduardo Villamor, Paul J. Catalano, Walter C. Willett, and Eric B. Rimm. 2014. "Few Changes in Food Security and Dietary Intake from Short-Term Participation in the Supplemental Nutrition Assistance Program Among Low-Income Massachusetts Adults." *Journal of Nutrition Education and Behavior* 46(1):68–74.

Leung, Cindy W., Eric L. Ding, Paul J. Catalano, Eduardo Villamor, Eric B. Rimm, and Walter C. Willett. 2012. "Dietary Intake and Dietary Quality of Low-Income Adults in the Supplemental Nutrition Assistance Program." *American Journal of Clinical Nutrition* 96(5):977–988.

Levedahl, J. William, Nicole Ballenger, and Courtney Harold. 1994. "Comparing the Emergency Food Assistance Program and the Food Stamp Program: Recipient Characteristics, Market Effects, and Benefit/Cost Ratios." Agricultural Economic Report for USDA Economic Research Service.

Litt, Jill S., Mah-J. Soobader, Mark S. Turbin, James W. Hale, Michael Buchenau, and Julie A. Marshall. 2011. "The Influence of Social Involvement, Neighborhood Aesthetics, and Community Garden Participation on

Fruit and Vegetable Consumption." *American Journal of Public Health* 101(8):1466–1473.

Lucan, Sean C., Frances K. Barg, Alison Karasz, Christina S. Palmer, and Judith A. Long. 2012. "Perceived Influences on Diet Among Urban, Low-Income, African-Americans." *American Journal of Health Behavior* 36(5):700–710.

Lucan, Sean C., Andrew R. Maroko, Omar Sanon, Rafael Frias, and Clyde B. Schechter. 2015. "Urban Farmers' Markets: Accessibility, Offerings, and Produce Variety, Quality, and Price Compared to Nearby Stores." *Appetite* 90(1):23–30.

Lynch, Elizabeth B., Shane Holmes, Kathryn Keim, and Sylvia A. Koneman. 2012. "Concepts of Healthful Food Among Low-Income African-American Women." *Journal of Nutrition Education and Behavior* 44(2):154–159.

Mabli, James, Emily S. Martin, and Laura Castner. 2010. "Effects of Economic Conditions and Program Policy on State Food Stamp Caseloads, 2000 to 2006." Princeton, NJ: Mathematica Policy Research.

Mackenzie, Annah, 2016. "Beyond Food: Community Gardens as Place of Connection and Empowerment." Project for Public Spaces. http://www.pps.org /article/beyond-food-community-gardens-as-places-of-connection-and -empowerment.

Marlette, Martha A., Susan B. Templeton, and Myna Panemangalore. 2005. "Food Type, Food Preparation, and Competitive Food Purchases Impact School Lunch Plate Waste by Sixth Grade Students." *Journal of the American Dietetic Association* 105(11):1779–1782.

Maslow, Abraham. 1943. "A Theory of Human Motivation." *Psychological Review* 50:370–396.

Maxwell, Simon. 1996. "Food Security: A Post-Modern Perspective." *Food Policy* 21(2):155–170.

McConnell, Sheena, Michael Ponza, and Rhoda R. Cohen. 1999. "Report on the Pretest of the Reaching the Working Poor and Poor Elderly Survey." Washington, DC: Mathematica Policy Research.

McKernan, Signe-Mary, Caroline E. Ratcliffe, and Emily Rosenberg. 2003. "Employment Factors Influencing Food Stamp Program Participation." Washington, DC: The Urban Institute.

McLaughlin, Katie A., Jennifer Greif Green, Margarita Alegría, E. Jane Costello, Michael J. Gruber, Nancy A. Sampson, and Ronald C. Kessler. 2012. "Food Insecurity and Mental Disorders in a National Sample of U.S. Adolescents." *Journal of the American Academy of Child Adolescent Psychiatry* 51(12):1293–1303.

Mello, Jennifer A., Kim M. Gans, Patricia Risicia, Usree Kirtania, Leslie Strolla, and Leanne Fournier. 2010. "How Is Food Insecurity Associated with Dietary Behaviors? An Analysis with Low Income, Ethnically Diverse Participants in a Nutrition Intervention Study." *Journal of the American Dietetic Association* 110:1906–1911.

Miller, Cyndee. 1994. "Rediscovering the Inner City." *Marketing News* 28(2):1–2.

Minkoff-Zern, Laura-Anne. 2012. "Knowing 'Good Food': Immigrant Knowledge and the Racial Politics of Farmworker Food Insecurity." *Antipode* 46(5): 1190–1204.

Mirtcheva, Donika M., and Lisa M. Powell. 2009. "Participation in the National School Lunch Program: Importance of School-Level and Neighborhood Contextual Factors." *Journal of School Health* 79(10):485–494.

Monsivais, Pablo, and Adam Drewnowski. 2007. "The Rising Cost of Low-Energy-Density Foods." *Journal of the American Dietetic Association* 107(12):2071–2076.

Morland, Kimberly, Steve Wing, and Ana Diez Roux. 2002. "The Contextual Effect of the Local Food Environment on Residents' Diets: The Atherosclerosis Risk in Communities Study." *American Journal of Public Health* 92(11):1761–1767.

Morrison, Rosanna Mentzer, and Lisa Mancino. 2015. "Most US Households Do Their Main Grocery Shopping." https://www.ers.usda.gov/amber-waves/2015/august/most-us-households-do-their-main-grocery-shopping-at-supermarkets-and-supercenters-regardless-of-income.

Nature Magazine. 2011. "Solutions for a Cultivated Planet." October. https://www.researchgate.net/publication/234112150_Solutions_for_a_Cultivated_Planet.

Newman, Constance, and Katherine Ralston. 2006. *Profiles of Participation in the National School Lunch Program: Data from Two National Surveys.* Economic Information Bulletin no. Number 17. http://ageconsearch.umn.edu/bitstream/7085/2/ei060017.pdf.

Nguyen, Binh T., Kerem Shuval, Valentine Y. Njike, and David L. Katz. 2014. "The Supplemental Nutrition Assistance Program and Dietary Quality Among US Adults: Findings from a Nationally Representative Survey." *Mayo Clinic Proceedings* 89(9):1211–1219.

Nguyen, Binh T., Kerem Shuval, Farryl Bertmann, and Amy L. Yaroch. 2015. "The Supplemental Nutrition Assistance Program, Food Insecurity, Dietary Quality, and Obesity Among US Adults." *American Journal of Public Health* 105(7):1453–1459.

Nord, Mark, and C. Philip Brent. 2002. "Food Insecurity in Higher Income Households." USDA Economic Research Service, Food Assistance and Nutrition Research Program, September.

Nyden, Philip, John Lukehart, Michael T. Maly, and William Peterman. 1998. "Neighborhood Racial and Ethnic Diversity in U.S. Cities." *Cityscape: A Journal of Policy Development and Research* 4(2):1–17.

Ohmer, Mary L., Pamela Meadowcraft, Kate Freed, and Ericka Lewis. 2009. "Community Gardening and Community Development: Individual, Social, and Community Benefits of a Community Conservation Program." *Journal of Community Practice* 17(4):377–399.

Older Americans Act. 2002. "The OAA Nutrition Programs." http://www.coalitionforaging.org/nutr.pdf.

Olster, Marjorie. 2013. "Key Points in the Genetically Modified Food Debate." *Yahoo! News,* August 2. http://news.yahoo.com/key-points-genetically-modified-food-debate-072020932.html.

Orange County Public Schools. 2014. "Operations: Service Efforts and Accomplishments, 2013–2014." https://www.ocps.net/op/Documents/2013-14%20Service%20Efforts%20and%20Accomplishments.pdf.

Owens, Nicole, and Amy Donley. 2015. "The Impact of the Farmers' Market Nutrition Program on Participating Florida Farmers: A Research Note." *Journal of Rural Social Science* 29(3):84–98.

Pan, Liping, Bettylou Sherry, Rashid Njai, and Heidi M. Blanck. 2012. "Food Insecurity Is Associated with Obesity Among US Adults in 12 States." *Journal of the Academy of Nutrition and Dietetics* 112:1403–1409.

Pardilla, Marla, Divya Prasad, Sonali Suratkar, and Joel Gittelsohn. 2014. "High Levels of Household Food Insecurity on the Navajo Nation." *Public Health Nutrition* 17(1):58–65.

Payette, Hélène, and Bryna Shatenstein. 2005. "Determinants of Healthy Eating in Community-Dwelling Elderly People." *Canadian Journal of Public Health* 96(S3):S27–S31.

Pearson, Tim, Jean M. Russell, Michael J. Campbell, and Margo E. Barker. 2005. Do 'Food Deserts' Influence Fruit and Vegetable Consumption?—A Cross-Sectional Study." *Appetite* 45:195–197.

Pheley Alfred M., David H. Holben, Annette S. Graham, and Chris Simpson. 2002. "Food Security and Perceptions of Health Status: A Preliminary Study in Rural Appalachia." *Journal of Rural Health* 18(3):447–454.

Ponza, Michael, James C. Ohls, and Barbara E. Millen. 1996. "Serving Elders at Risk: National Evaluation of the Elderly Nutrition Program, 1993–1995." Princeton: Mathematica Policy Research.

Poppendieck, Janet. 1999. *Sweet Charity? Emergency Food and the End of Entitlement.* London: Penguin.

Potamites, Elizabeth, and Anne Gordon. 2010. "Children's Food Security and Intakes from School Meals: Final Report." Mathematica Policy Research. http://naldc.nal.usda.gov/download/42320/pdf.

Powell, Lisa M., M. Christopher Auld, Frank J. Chaloupka, Patrick M. O'Malley, and Lloyd D. Johnston. 2007b. "Access to Fast Food and Food Prices: The Relationship with Fruit and Vegetable Consumption and Overweight Status Among Adolescents." *Advanced Health and Economic Health Services Research* 17:23–48.

Powell, Lisa M., Sandy Slater, Donka Mirtcheva, Yanjun Bao, and Frank J. Chaloupka. 2007a. "Food Store Availability and Neighborhood Characteristics in the United States." *Preventive Medicine* 44(3):189–195.

Pringle, Peter (ed.). 2013. *A Place at the Table.* New York: PublicAffairs.

Radimer, Kathy L., Christine M. Olson, and Cathy C. Campbell. 1990. "Development of Indicators to Assess Hunger." *Journal of Nutrition* 120(S11):1544–1548.

Radimer, Kathy L., Christine M. Olson, Jennifer C. Greene, Cathy C. Campbell, and Jean-Pierre Habicht. 1992. "Understanding Hunger and Developing Indicators to Assess It in Women and Children." *Journal of Nutrition Education* 24(1):S36–S44.

Rao, Mayuree, Ashkan Afshin, Gitanjali Singh, and Dariush Mozaffarian. 2013. "Do Healthier Foods and Diet Patterns Cost More Than Less Healthy Options? A Systematic Review and Meta-Analysis." *BMJ Open.* http://dx.doi.org/10.1136/bmjopen-2013-004277.

Rice, Xan. 2011. "Hunger Pains: Famine in the Horn of Africa." *The Guardian,* August 8. https://www.theguardian.com/global-development/2011/aug/08/hunger-pains-famine-horn-africa.

Roseman, Mary, and Jessica R. Niblock. 2006. "A Culinary Approach to Healthy Menu Items: Middle School Students' Opinion of School Lunch and Lunch Decision Factors." *Journal of Culinary Science and Technology* 5(1):75–90.

Rosenbaum, Dottie. 2013. "SNAP Is Effective and Efficient." Washington, DC: Center on Budget and Policy Priorities.

Rosier, Kate. 2011. "Food Insecurity in Australia: What Is It, Who Experiences It, and How Can Child and Family Services Support Families Experiencing It?" CAFCA Practice Sheet. https://aifs.gov.au/cfca/publications/food-insecurity-australia-what-it-who-experiences-it.

Roy, Marie-Andrée, and Hélène Payette. 2006. "Meals-On-Wheels Improves Energy and Nutrient Intake in a Frail Free-Living Elderly Population." *Journal of Nutrition Health & Aging* 10(6):554–560.

Ruopeng, An, and Roland Sturm. 2012. "School and Residential Neighborhood Food Environment and Diet Among California Youth." *American Journal of Preventive Medicine* 42(2):129–135.

Sallis, James F., and Karen Glanz. 2006. "The Role of Built Environments in Physical Activity, Eating, and Obesity in Childhood." *Future of Children: Childhood Obesity* 16(1):89–108.

Sanders, Bernard. 2011. *Senior Hunger: The Human Toll and Consequences.* http://www.sanders.senate.gov/imo/media/doc/SeniorHungerReport.pdf.

Sanger-Katz, Margot. 2015. "Giving the Poor Easy Access to Healthy Food Doesn't Mean They'll Buy It." *New York Times,* May 18. http://www.nytimes.com/2015/05/09/upshot/giving-the-poor-easy-access-to-healthy-food-doesnt-mean-theyll-buy-it.html?_r=0.

Schmelzkopf, Karen. 1995. "Urban Community Gardens as Contested Space." *Geographical Review* 85(3):364–381.

Seligman, Hilary K., Terry C. Davis, Dean Schillinger, and Michael S. Wolf. 2010. "Food Insecurity Is Associated with Hypoglycemia and Poor Diabetes Self-Management in a Low-Income Sample with Diabetes." *Journal of Health Care for the Poor and Underserved* 21:1227–1233.

Seligman, Hilary K., Elizabeth A. Jacobs, Andrea Lopez, Urmimala Sarkar, Jeanne Tschann, and Alicia Fernandez. 2011. "Food Insecurity and Hypoglycemia Among Safety Net Patients with Diabetes." *Archives of Internal Medicine* 171:1204–1206.

Sen, Amartya. 1981. *Poverty and Famines: An Essay on Entitlement and Deprivation.* Oxford: Clarendon.

Sen, Amartya, and Jean Drèze. Eds. 1991. *The Political Economy of Hunger.* 3 vols. Oxford: Clarendon.

Shaffer, Amanda. 2002. "The Persistence of L.A.'s Grocery Gap: The Need for a New Food Policy and Approach to Market Development." http://scholar.oxy.edu/uep_faculty/16.

Shenkin, Jonathan D., and Michael F. Jacobson. 2010. "Using the Food Stamp Program and Other Methods to Promote Healthy Diets for Low-Income Consumers." *American Journal of Public Health* 100(9):1562–1564.

Shetty, Prakash. 2002. *Nutrition Through the Life Cycle.* London: Royal Society of Chemistry.

Shier, Victoria, An Ruopeng, and Roland Sturm. 2012. "Is There a Robust Relationship Between Neighbourhood Food Environment and Childhood Obesity in the USA?" *Public Health* 126(9):723–730.

Short, Anne, Julie Guthman, and Samuel Raskin. 2007. "Food Deserts, Oases, or Mirages?" *Journal of Planning Education and Research* 26:352–364.

Slusser, Wendelin, Jennifer Toller Erausquin, Michael Prelip, Heidi Fischer, William G. Cumberland, Fred Frankel, and Charlotte Newman. 2012. "Nutrition Knowledge and Behaviours of Low-Income Latino Parents of Preschoolers: Associations with Nutrition-Related Parenting Practices." *Early Child Development and Care* 182(8):1041–1055.

Smith, Stephanie L., and Leslie Cunningham-Sabo. 2013. "Food Choice, Plate Waste, and Nutrient Intake of Elementary- and Middle-School Students Participating in the U.S. National School Lunch Program." *Public Health Nutrition* 17(6):1255–1263.

Smith-Spangler, Crystal, Margaret L. Brandeau, Grace E. Hunter, J. Clay Bavinger, Maren Pearson, Paul J. Eschbach, Vandana Sundaram, Hau Liu,

Patricia Schirmer, Christopher Stave, Ingram Olkin, and Dena M. Bravata. 2012. "Are Organic Foods Safer or Healthier Than Conventional Alternatives? A Systematic Review." *Annals of Internal Medicine* 157(5):348–366.

Solzhenitsyn, Aleksandr. 1963. *One Day in the Life of Ivan Denisovich: A Novel.* New York: Dutton.

Song, Hee-Jung, Stephanie K. Grutzmacher, and Jane Kostenko. 2014. "Personal Weight Status Classification and Health Literacy Among Supplemental Nutrition Assistance Program (SNAP) Participants." *Journal of Community Health* 39(3):446–453.

Sparks, Andrea, Neil Bania, and Laura Leete. 2011. "Comparative Approaches to Measuring Food Access in Urban Areas: The Case of Portland, Oregon." *Urban Studies* 48:1715–1737.

Spiertz, J. H. J. 2010. "Nitrogen, Sustainable Agriculture, and Food Security: A Review." *Agronomy for Sustainable Development* 30(1):43–55.

Stone, Chad, Arloc Sherman, and Brynne Keith-Jennings. 2015. "No Mystery Why SNAP Enrollment Remains High: It's Still the Economy." Washington, DC: Center on Budget and Policy Priorities, March.

Strickhouser, Sara M. 2016. *Food Insecurity, Social Inequality, and Social Policy.* Unpublished PhD dissertation, University of Central Florida, Department of Sociology.

Strickhouser, Sara, James D. Wright, and Amy M. Donley. 2015. "Food Insecurity Among Older Adults: 2014 Update." AARP Foundation. http://www.aarp.org/content/dam/aarp/aarp_foundation/2015-PDFs/AF-Food-Insecurity-2015Update-Final-Report.pdf.

Stuff, Janice E., Patrick H. Casey, Kitty L. Szeto, Jeffrey M. Gossett, James M. Robbins, Pippa M. Simpson, Carol Connell, and Margaret L. Bogle. 2004. "Household Food Insecurity Is Associated with Adult Health Status." *Journal of Nutrition* 134:2330–2335.

Swanson, Mark. 2008. "Digital Photography as a Tool to Measure School Cafeteria Consumption." *Journal of School Health* 78(8):432–437.

Talbot, David. 2015. "Megascale Desalination." *MIT Technology Review* http://www.technologyreview.com/featuredstory/534996/megascale-desalination.

Tam, Benita Y., Leanne Findlay, and Dafna Kohen. 2014. "Social Networks as a Coping Strategy for Food Insecurity and Hunger for Young Aboriginal and Canadian Children." *Societies* 4(3):1–14.

Tarasuk, Valerie. 2001. "Household Food Insecurity with Hunger Is Associated with Woman's Food Intakes, Health, and Household Circumstances." *Journal of Nutrition* 131:2670–2676.

Taylor, Ashley P. 2015. "The One Food Myth We Were Totally Wrong About." http://www.refinery29.com/2015/05/87956/new-york-health-food-deserts.

Taylor, John R., and Sarah Taylor Lovell. 2015. "Urban Home Gardens in the Global North: A Mixed Methods Study of Ethnic and Migrant Home Gardens in Chicago, IL." *Renewable Agriculture and Food Systems* 30:22–32.

Thomas, Lionel, Jr., Richard Ghiselli, and Barbara Almanza. 2011. "Congregate Meal Sites Participants: Can They Manage Their Diets?" *International Journal of Hospitality Management* 30:31–37.

Tiehen, Laura, Dean Joliffe, and Craig Gunderson. 2012. "Alleviating Poverty in the United States: The Critical Role of SNAP Benefits." Economic Research Report Number 132. Washington, DC: US Department of Agriculture.

To, Quyen G., Edward A. Frongillo, Danielle Gallegos, and Justin B. Moore. 2014. "Household Food Insecurity Is Associated with Less Physical Activity

Among Children and Adults in the U.S. Population." *Journal of Nutrition* 144(11):1797–1802.

Tomlinson, Isobel. 2011. "Doubling Food Production to Feed the 9 Billion: A Critical Perspective on a Key Discourse of Food Security in the UK." *Journal of Rural Studies* 29:81–90.

Topeka Capital Journal. 2014. "Editorial: What Good Are School Lunches If Kids Won't Eat Them?" July 15. http://cjonline.com/opinion/2014-07-15 /editorial-what-good-are-school-lunches-if-kids-wont-eat-them.

Townsend, Marilyn S., Janet Peerson, Bradley Love, Cheryl Achterberg, and Suzanne P. Murphy. 2001. "Food Insecurity Is Positively Related to Overweight in Women." *Journal of Nutrition* 131(6):1738–1745.

Tussing-Humphreys, Lisa, Jessica L. Thomson, Tanyatta Mayo, and Emanuel Edmond. 2013. "A Church-Based Diet and Physical Activity Intervention for Rural, Lower Mississippi Delta African-American Adults: Delta Body and Soul Effectiveness Study, 2010–2011." *Preventing Chronic Disease.* http:// dx.doi.org/10.5888/pcd10.120286.

United Nations. 2009. "Food Production Must Double by 2050 to Meet Demand from World's Growing Population, Innovative Strategies Needed to Combat Hunger, Experts Tell Second Committee." http://www.un.org/press/en/2009 /gaef3242.doc.htm.

United Nations Environment Programme (UNEP). 2010. "Assessing the Environmental Impacts of Consumption and Production: Priority Products and Materials." Report of the Working Group on the Environmental Impacts of Products and Materials to the International Panel for Sustainable Resource Management.

United Nations Food and Agricultural Organization (FAO). 2009. "How to Feed the World in 2050." Paper prepared for the High-Level Expert Forum, Rome, 12–19 October. http://www.fao.org/fileadmin/templates/wsfs/docs/expert _paper/How_to_Feed_the_World_in_2050.pdf.

US Census Bureau. 2017. "Income and Poverty in the United States: 2016." https:// census.gov/content/dam/Census/library/publications/2017/demo/P60-259.pdf.

US Department of Agriculture. 2009. "Access to Affordable and Nutritious Food Measuring and Understanding Food Deserts and Their Consequences: Report to Congress." Washington, DC: US Government Printing Office.

———. 2011. "Benefit Redemption Patterns in the Supplemental Nutrition Assistance Program: Final Report." http://www.fns.usda.gov/benefit-redemption -patterns-supplemental-nutrition-assistance-program.

———. 2012. "School Breakfast Program." http://www.fns.usda.gov/sites/default /files/sbpfactsheet.pdf.

———. 2013. "Food Deserts." http://apps.ams.usda.gov/fooddeserts/foodDeserts.aspx.

———. 2014. "School Meals: Provisions 1, 2, and 3." http://www.fns.usda.gov/school -meals/provisions-1-2-and-3.

———. 2015a. "National School Lunch Program: Participation and Lunches Served." http://www.fns.usda.gov/sites/default/files/pd/slsummar.pdf.

———. 2015b. "School Breakfast Program Participation and Meals Served." http://www.fns.usda.gov/sites/default/files/pd/sbsummar.pdf.

———. 2016. "Supplemental Nutrition Assistance Program (SNAP)." http:// www.fns.usda.gov/pd/supplemental-nutrition-assistance-program-snap.

Van der Ploeg, Jan Douwe. 2015. "Peasantry in the Twenty-First Century." In James D. Wright (ed.), *The International Encyclopedia of the Social and Behavioral Sciences,* 2nd ed., volume 17, 664–668. Oxford: Elsevier.

Walker, Renee, Jason Block, and Ichiro Kawachi. 2012. "Do Residents of Food Deserts Express Different Food Buying Preferences Compared to Residents of Food Oases? A Mixed-Methods Analysis." *International Journal of Behavioral Nutrition and Physical Activity* 9:41–54.

Walker, Renee E., Christopher R. Keane, and Jessica G. Burke. 2010. "Disparities and Access to Healthy Food in the United States: A Review of Food Deserts Literature." *Health and Place* 16:876–884.

Webb, Amy L., Andrew Schiff, Douglas Currivan, and Eduardo Villamor. 2008. "Food Stamp Program Participation but Not Food Insecurity Is Associated with Higher Adult BMI in Massachusetts Residents Living in Low-Income Neighbourhoods." *Public Health Nutrition* 11(12):1248–1255.

Wellman, Nancy S. 2010. "Aging at Home: More Research on Nutrition and Independence, Please." *American Journal of Clinical Nutrition* 91(5):1151–1152.

Wells, Jennie L., and Andrea C. Dumbrell. 2006. "Nutrition and Aging: Assessment and Treatment of Compromised Nutritional Status in Frail Elderly Patients." *Clinical Interventions in Aging* 1(1):67–79.

Whitaker, Robert C., Shannon M. Phillips, and Sean M. Orzol. 2006. "Food Insecurity and the Risks of Depression and Anxiety in Mothers and Behavior Problems in Their Preschool-Aged Children." *Pediatrics* 118(3):e859–e868.

White, Martin. 2007. "Food Access and Obesity." *Obesity Reviews* 8:99–107.

Wienk, Ronald E. 1979. "Measuring Racial Discrimination in American Housing Markets: The Housing Market Practices Survey." Washington, DC: US Department of Housing and Urban Development.

Wilde, Parke. 2013. *Food Policy in the United States: An Introduction.* New York: Routledge.

Wilde, Parke E., and Christine K. Ranney. 2000. "The Monthly Food-Stamp Cycle: Shopping Frequency and Food Intake Decisions in an Endogenous Switching Regression Framework." *American Journal of Agricultural Economics* 82:200–213.

Winne, Mark. 2008. *Closing the Food Gap: Resetting the Table in the Land of Plenty.* Boston: Beacon.

Worldometers. n.d. "The World Population at 7 Billion." http://www.worldometers.info/world-population.

Wrigley, Neil, Daniel Warm, and Barrie Margetts. 2002. "Assessing the Impact of Improved Retail Access on Diet in a 'Food Desert': A Preliminary Report." *Urban Studies* 39:2061–2082.

Wutich, Amber, and Alexandra Brewis. 2014. "Food, Water, and Scarcity: Toward a Broader Anthropology of Resource Insecurity." *Current Anthropology* 55(4):444–468.

Zenk, Shannon N., and Lisa M. Powell. 2008. "U.S. Secondary Schools and Food Outlets." *Health and Place* 14:336–346.

Zenk, Shannon N., Amy J. Schulz, Barbara A. Israel, Sherman A. James, Shuming Bao, and Mark L. Wilson. 2005. "Neighborhood Racial Composition, Neighborhood Poverty, and the Spatial Accessibility of Supermarkets in Metropolitan Detroit." *American Journal of Public Health* 95(4):660–667.

Zhu, Huichen, and An Ruopeng. 2013. "Impact of Home-Delivered Meal Programs on Diet and Nutrition Among Older Adults." *Nutrition and Health* 22(2):89–103.

Ziliak, James P., and Craig Gunderson. 2011. "Food Insecurity Among Older Adults." AARP Foundation. http://www.aarp.org/content/dam/aarp/aarp_foundation /pdf_2011/AARPFoundation_HungerReport_2011.pdf.

Ziliak, James P., Craig Gunderson, and Margaret Haist. 2008. "The Consequences, Causes, and Future of Senior Hunger in America." http://www.mowaa.org /document.doc?id=13.

Index

About the Book

In the United States today, 50 million people don't have enough food. How is this possible in one of the world's wealthiest countries? Why hasn't the problem been solved? Is it simply an economic issue? Challenging conventional wisdom, the authors of *Hunger in the Land of Plenty* explore the causes and consequences of food insecurity; assess some of the major policies and programs that have been designed to reduce it; and consider alternative paths forward.

James D. Wright is Provost's Distinguished Research Professor Emeritus and Pegasus Professor Emeritus in the Department of Sociology at the University of Central Florida. **Amy Donley** is associate professor of sociology at the University of Central Florida. **Sara Strickhouser Vega** is president of Vega Nguyen Research and also teaches sociology at Western Washington University.